Good Food Ideas
Cheese Cookbook
from KRAFT

A Benjamin Company Book

Pictured on the cover —

Classic Cheesecake

Quiche Lorraine

Homesteader's Casserole

Table of Contents

From Our Kitchens To Yours

Cheese! What was discovered by chance centuries ago has become an international food favorite. Why? Because cheese is versatile. It's appropriate for any menu — morning, noon, night and in-between; for guests; for family. It's convenient and nutritious. Almost everyone likes it — young or old, rich or poor. No wonder people smile when they say cheese!

Written for cheeseburger fans as well as soufflé gourmets, this book is all about cheese, from legend and history, to making, to market, to kitchen, to table. In the chapters that follow, you'll find facts, quick and easy tips and recipes for all kinds of cheese dishes created by the home economists from the Kraft Kitchens. It's the best of their Good Food Cheese Ideas.

Filling the pages are almost 400 recipes from Appetizers to Zesty vegetables. All are tested and designed for today's lifestyle.

So go ahead. Explore the magic of the microwave. Visit cheese countries around the world. And take our cheese and wine mini-course to learn how to select and serve these perfect partners.

Dorothy Holland
Director, The Kraft Kitchens

Introduction

CHEESE MADE SIMPLE

Imagine, if you can, a trip to your local supermarket, accompanied by your great grandmother. She would recognize some things in the dairy case like milk, eggs and butter, although the containers might be unfamiliar. But the wondrous assortment of cheeses would surely be bewildering. There is such an infinite variety of cheese available in almost every corner of the United States today that we have come to take its availability for granted. And because there is such a magnificent assortment of cheeses to choose from, shopping for cheese can be confusing unless you understand what the different cheeses are, the taste variations you are likely to find, the many ways in which cheese can be used, how to buy cheese, how to cook with cheese and how to store it. This book is intended to help provide you with the information you need to become a knowledgeable cheese shopper. You'll find a large selection of delicious, kitchen-tested recipes that will help you plan and cook new and exciting meals for your family and friends.

BUYING CHEESE

Natural cheese and process cheese products are found in or near the refrigerated dairy case in most supermarkets. Since cheese fits into two of the basic food groups — the milk group and the meat group — you'll want to include it in your daily menus. Cheese products supply many of the nutritional needs of your family, as well as being delicious taste treats appropriate at any time of day.

Natural cheeses are always stored in the dairy case in a tempting array of distinctive shapes. You can choose from among wedges, wheels, balls, flat rounds, sticks and convenient packaged slices.

Pasteurized process cheese food and spreads are also available in a wide variety of shapes and flavors: slices, loaves, links, dips and spreads. The process cheese products that don't require refrigeration — in glasses, loaves, and squeeze packs — are usually found above or near the dairy case.

It's easy to become familiar with cheeses you have never tasted. Just make it a practice to buy a small quantity of a new cheese when you stop at the dairy case. If you and your family enjoy the taste of the "new" cheese, you can buy a larger quantity the next time you shop, and then go on to try another unfamiliar cheese.

An open, or freshness, date appears on the label of all Kraft cheeses. Be sure to look for the statement "Best when purchased by (date)." This date assures peak flavor and freshness at the time of your purchase and for a reasonable period after that date when kept under accepted home conditions.

STORING CHEESE

When you store unopened cheese at home, consult the label on the package for helpful instructions, or follow the example of your grocer and keep the cheese in the same way it was stored in the supermarket. Since most cheese is kept in the dairy case, this is your clue that cheese should also be refrigerated at home. Jars and loaves of cheese that are kept on non-refrigerated shelves in the supermarket may be stored at room temperature at home until you are ready to use them. Once they are opened, they should be kept in the refrigerator. There are some exceptions, however. Products such as squeeze packs should *never* be refrigerated. They'll stay fresh at room temperature for as long as they last.

"Keep air out and moisture in" is a good rule to remember when storing cheese. Reseal unused portions of cheese in the original wrapping, or use foil, transparent wrap or plastic bags wrapped snug and tight around the cheese to keep it moist and fresh. The wrapping around single slices of cheese, carefully designed foil packaging materials, and easy-to-open-and-reseal plastic lids and metal caps are all specially designed to keep cheese products fresh.

TO FREEZE OR NOT TO FREEZE

Cheese will keep a relatively long period of time at refrigerator temperature if it is properly wrapped. You can freeze cheese to extend its storage life, but freezing may adversely affect body and texture. Frozen cheese occasionally becomes crumbly or mealy, in which case it is best-suited for use in cooking.

If you want to freeze cheese, seal it tightly in a moisture-proof material such as plastic wrap or foil especially designed for freezing. Cheeses like Cheddar, Swiss, Edam or Gouda may be stored in the freezer if they are frozen rapidly in small (half pound) packages. If cheese has been cut into small cubes, it should not be kept in the freezer longer than three weeks. Slices and loaves of natural cheese such as Cheddar and Swiss, as well as pasteurized process cheese products, may be kept frozen for up to three months. Before you use frozen cheese, thaw it slowly, preferably in the refrigerator, while it is still wrapped.

CORRECT TEMPERATURE TO SERVE CHEESE

The flavor and character of most cheeses come through best when cheese is served at room temperature. In order to bring out the best flavor in cheese, remove it from the refrigerator at least thirty minutes before you plan to serve it. Cheeses like Camembert should be soft and almost runny. Take them out of the refrigerator at least two hours before serving. Among the cheeses which should *not* be served at room temperature are cottage cheese, Neufchatel and cream cheese. They should always be served chilled.

HOW MUCH CHEESE?

1 cup grated, shredded or cubed cheese = 4 ounces
1/2 cup grated, shredded or cubed cheese = 2 ounces
1/4 cup grated, shredded or cubed cheese = 1 ounce

When a recipe calls for a specific quantity of cheese, use the above guide to determine the amount of cheese to buy or prepare. This guide applies to both natural and process cheeses.

COOKING WITH CHEESE

Cheese, like all protein food, is adversely affected by high heat or prolonged cooking. Although pasteurized process cheese products are less susceptible to heat than natural cheese, you should follow two rules when cooking cheese:

Use low to medium heat.

Do not overcook. Heat just until cheese melts.

For best results when cooking, follow these hints:

• Shred natural cheese when it is to be melted in sauces, in toppings or mixed with other food. (You can buy cheese already shredded, packed in convenient packages.)

• Cube process cheese when adding it to other food. It will melt quickly and blend easily.

• When making a cheese sauce: add cheese just before the sauce is finished and heat only until melted.

• When broiling: place pan several inches below the source of the heat and broil only until cheese melts.

• When using cheese in baked dishes: bake at low to moderate temperature (325°F to 375°F).

• When topping a casserole: place cheese on top of the casserole during the last few minutes of baking only.

• Most parmesan-type cheeses are sold already grated or shredded. Grated cheese is finer and drier than shredded cheese.

• Cream cheese and Neufchatel will blend readily with other ingredients if they are allowed to soften for at least 30 minutes at room temperature before they are used.

A LAST WORD

Kraft's continuing experimentation and research have produced an ever-increasing number of wonderful products. The names of these products have become household words and their flavors and many properties of slicing, shredding, melting, grating, and spreading, delight cooks everywhere. Pasteurized process cheese food in glasses, a wide variety of ready-sliced cheese in packages, cream cheese that is guaranteed to be fresh when purchased, individually wrapped cheese and process cheese slices — these are only a few of Kraft's contributions to the ease of food preparation, the ease of serving food, and the joy of eating in American homes.

— **The Editors**

Opposite: Super Cheddar Spread (page 16), Petite Quiches (page 16)

Chapter 1
Sociable Snacks

Super Cheddar Spread

2 cups (8 ounces) shredded Kraft
  sharp natural cheddar cheese
1/4 cup Parkay margarine
2 teaspoons chili sauce

1/2 teaspoon Worcestershire sauce
4 crisply cooked bacon slices,
  crumbled

Combine cheese, margarine, chili sauce and Worcestershire sauce, mixing until well blended. Stir in bacon. 1 3/4 cups

Variation: To make a dip instead, stir in 1 tablespoon of milk.

Petite Quiches

Pastry for 9-inch unbaked pie crust
3/4 cup half and half
2 eggs, slightly beaten
1/4 teaspoon salt
Dash of pepper

1 cup (4 ounces) Kraft shredded
  natural Swiss cheese
1 tablespoon flour
4 crisply cooked bacon slices,
  crumbled

Line ungreased miniature muffin pans with pastry. Combine half and half, eggs and seasonings; mix well. Toss cheese with flour; add cheese and bacon to egg mixture. Fill muffin shells two-thirds full with egg and cheese mixture. Bake at 325°, 30 to 35 minutes or until lightly browned. 2 dozen

Variation: Line an 8-inch square baking dish with pastry, placing it across the bottom and 1 inch up the sides. Pour egg and cheese mixture into pastry shell. Bake at 325⁰, 40 to 45 minutes or until lightly browned.

Make a "Colby Spiral" for an attractive addition to a cheese tray by cutting a 16-ounce longhorn style natural colby cheese crosswise into 8 slices. Turn upright and cut vertically into quarters. Serve with party picks.

"Philly" Shrimp Dip

1 8-ounce package Philadelphia
  Brand cream cheese
2 tablespoons milk

1 4 1/2-ounce can shrimp,
  drained, rinsed
2 teaspoons lemon juice
Dash of Worcestershire sauce

Combine softened cream cheese and milk, mixing until well blended. Add remaining ingredients; mix well. 1 1/2 cups

Garlic Dip

1 8-ounce package Philadelphia
   Brand cream cheese
1/4 cup milk

1 teaspoon lemon juice
1 garlic clove, minced
1/2 teaspoon seasoned salt

Combine softened cream cheese with remaining ingredients, mixing until well blended. 1 1/4 cups

Clam Appetizer Dip

1 8-ounce can minced clams
1 garlic clove, cut in half
1 8-ounce package Philadelphia
   Brand cream cheese
2 teaspoons lemon juice

1 1/2 teaspoons Worcestershire
   sauce
1/2 teaspoon salt
Dash of pepper

Drain clams, reserving 1/4 cup liquid. Rub mixing bowl with garlic. Combine softened cream cheese, clams, reserved clam liquid and remaining ingredients, mixing until well blended. Chill.
1 2/3 cups

Tempting Cheese Ball

1 8-ounce package Philadelphia
   Brand cream cheese
2 5-ounce jars Old English sharp
   pasteurized process cheese
   spread

1/2 cup (2 ounces) Kraft cold
   pack blue cheese
1 tablespoon finely chopped onion
1 tablespoon Worcestershire sauce
Chopped fresh parsley

Combine softened cream cheese, cheese spread and blue cheese, mixing until well blended. Add onion and Worcestershire sauce; mix well. Chill. Shape into a ball; roll in parsley. 1 ball

---

Add extra zest to popcorn by tossing it with melted margarine and grated parmesan cheese. Use approximately 1/4 cup (1 ounce) of parmesan cheese with 8 cups of popped popcorn.

Sherried Edam Spread

1 12-ounce Kraft natural edam
   cheese
2 tablespoons soft Parkay
   margarine

2 tablespoons sherry
1/4 cup chopped pecans

Slice top from cheese. Remove cheese from center, leaving 1/2-inch shell. Combine cheese, margarine and sherry, mixing until well blended. Stir in nuts. Fill shell.

"Philly" Cheese Bell

1 8-ounce package Cracker Barrel
  brand sharp cheddar flavor
  cold pack cheese food
1 8-ounce package Philadelphia
  Brand cream cheese
Parkay margarine

2 teaspoons chopped pimiento
2 teaspoons chopped green pepper
2 teaspoons chopped onion
1 teaspoon Worcestershire sauce
1/2 teaspoon lemon juice

Combine cold pack cheese food, softened cream cheese and 2 tablespoons margarine; mix until well blended. Add remaining ingredients; mix well. Mold into bell shapes, using 2 cold pack containers coated with margarine or lined with plastic wrap. Chill until firm. Unmold and garnish with chopped fresh parsley and pimiento strips, if desired.   2 bells

Mexicali Spread

1 8-ounce package Cracker Barrel
  brand sharp cheddar flavor
  cold pack cheese food
1 8-ounce package Philadelphia
  Brand cream cheese

1 tablespoon chopped green
  chili pepper
1 teaspoon chili powder
1 teaspoon chopped pimiento

Combine cold pack cheese food and softened cream cheese, mix until well blended. Add remaining ingredients; mix well. Mold into 2 cold pack containers coated with margarine or lined with plastic wrap. Chill until firm. Unmold and garnish with crushed corn chips, if desired.   2 molds

Horseradish Ham Dip

1 8-ounce package Philadelphia
  Brand cream cheese
3/4 cup finely chopped cooked
  ham

1/4 cup milk
1 tablespoon cream-style prepared
  horseradish
Dash of salt and pepper

Combine softened cream cheese, ham, milk, horseradish and seasonings; mix until well blended.   2 cups

Opposite: "Philly" Cheese Bell, Mexicali Spread

Creamy Cheddar Dip

1 8-ounce package Philadelphia
  Brand cream cheese
1/4 cup milk
1/4 cup Kraft real mayonnaise

1 cup (4 ounces) shredded
  Cracker Barrel brand sharp
  natural cheddar cheese
2 tablespoons chopped chives
1/4 teaspoon onion salt

Combine softened cream cheese, milk and mayonnaise, mixing until well blended. Add remaining ingredients; mix well. Chill. 2 cups

> Another easy dip is made by combining an 8-ounce jar of Cheez Whiz pasteurized process cheese spread with 1/2 cup of dairy sour cream.

Party Cheese Ball

2 8-ounce packages Philadelphia
  Brand cream cheese
2 cups (8 ounces) shredded
  Cracker Barrel brand sharp
  natural cheddar cheese
1 tablespoon chopped pimiento
1 tablespoon chopped green
  pepper

1 tablespoon finely chopped onion
2 teaspoons Worcestershire sauce
1 teaspoon lemon juice
Dash of cayenne
Dash of salt
Finely chopped pecans

Combine softened cream cheese and cheddar cheese, mixing until well blended. Add pimiento, green pepper, onion, Worcestershire sauce, lemon juice and seasonings; mix well. Chill. Shape into a ball; roll in nuts.   1 ball

Variation: Omit pecans; roll in finely chopped fresh parsley, chopped dried beef or toasted chopped almonds.

Frosted Party Ball

1 12-ounce can luncheon meat,
  finely chopped
1/4 cup Miracle Whip salad
  dressing
1/2 cup (2 ounces) Kraft grated
  parmesan cheese

2 tablespoons chopped onion
1 tablespoon sweet pickle relish
          *   *   *
1 3-ounce package Philadelphia
  Brand cream cheese
1 tablespoon milk

Combine luncheon meat and salad dressing, mixing at medium speed on electric mixer until well blended. Add parmesan cheese, onion and pickle relish; mix well. Chill. Shape into a ball.
Combine softened cream cheese and milk, mixing until well blended. Frost chilled ball.   1 ball

Creamy Appetizer Spread

1 8-ounce package Philadelphia
   Brand cream cheese
1 5-ounce jar Roka blue brand
   pasteurized cheese spread
1 5-ounce jar Old English sharp
   pasteurized process cheese
   spread

2 tablespoons finely chopped onion
1 garlic clove, minced
Chopped fresh parsley

Combine softened cream cheese and process cheese spreads, mixing until well blended. Add onion and garlic; mix well. Chill. Shape into a ball; roll in parsley.   1 ball

Variation: Substitute 2 tablespoons finely chopped green pepper for garlic clove. Omit parsley and roll ball in crushed potato chips.

Crown Cheese Ball

1 8-ounce package Philadelphia
   Brand cream cheese
2 cups (8 ounces) shredded
   Cracker Barrel brand sharp
   natural cheddar cheese

1/4 cup milk
1 3 1/2-ounce can French fried
   onions, crushed
1/3 cup chopped stuffed green
   olives

Combine softened cream cheese, cheddar cheese and milk, mixing until well blended. Reserve 1/2 cup onions. Stir in remaining onions and olives. Chill. Shape into a ball; roll in reserved onions. Garnish with stuffed green olive slices, if desired.   1 ball

---

To make a dip that's hot and hearty, combine an 8-ounce jar of Cheez Whiz pasteurized process cheese spread and an 11 1/2-ounce can of condensed bean with bacon soup. Heat and serve with corn chips.

"Philly" Stuffed Mushrooms

1 pound medium mushrooms
Parkay margarine
1 8-ounce package Philadelphia
   Brand cream cheese

1/4 cup (1 ounce) Kraft cold
   pack blue cheese, crumbled
2 tablespoons chopped onion

Remove stems of mushrooms; chop enough stems to make 1/2 cup. Sauté mushroom caps in margarine 5 minutes. Combine softened cream cheese and blue cheese, mixing until well blended. Stir in chopped stems and onion. Fill mushroom caps; broil until golden brown.   Approximately 2 1/2 dozen

Stuffed Mushrooms Parma

1 pound medium mushrooms
1/2 cup (2 ounces) Kraft grated
   parmesan cheese

1/4 cup Parkay margarine, melted
1 tablespoon chopped green onion

Remove stems of mushrooms; chop stems. Combine stems, cheese, margarine and onion. Fill mushroom caps. Place on rack of broiler pan; broil 2 to 3 minutes or until top of filling is slightly crusty. Serve hot.   Approximately 2 1/2 dozen

Toasty Onion Roll-Ups

White bread slices
Cheez Whiz pasteurized process
   cheese spread

Green onions
Soft Parkay margarine

For each snack, trim crusts from bread; cover with process cheese spread. Place onion at edge of bread; roll up. Spread bread rolls with margarine; broil until lightly browned.

Creole Canapés

1 3-ounce package Philadelphia
   Brand cream cheese
2 tablespoons catsup
5 crisply cooked bacon slices,
   crumbled

1 teaspoon finely chopped onion
1/2 teaspoon Worcestershire sauce
24 1 1/2-inch bread rounds,
   toasted

Combine softened cream cheese and catsup, mixing until well blended. Add bacon, onion and Worcestershire sauce; mix well. Spread rounds with cheese mixture. Broil until hot. Serve immediately.   2 dozen

Regal Spread

1 8-ounce package Cracker Barrel
   brand sharp cheddar flavor
   cold pack cheese food

1 8-ounce package Philadelphia
   Brand cream cheese
1/2 cup chopped pecans
1 tablespoon sherry

Combine cold pack cheese food and softened cream cheese; mix until well blended. Add remaining ingredients; mix well. Mold into 2 cold pack containers coated with margarine or lined with plastic wrap. Chill until firm. Unmold and garnish with chopped pecans, if desired.   2 molds

Crispy Cheese Wafers

2 cups (8 ounces) shredded Kraft   1 teaspoon Worcestershire sauce
  sharp natural cheddar cheese   1/4 teaspoon salt
1/2 cup Parkay margarine   1 cup flour

Combine cheese and margarine; stir in Worcestershire sauce and salt. Add flour; mix well. Form dough into two rolls, 1 1/2-inches in diameter. Wrap tightly; chill several hours or overnight. Cut dough into thin slices. Place on greased cookie sheet; bake at 375°, 10 minutes.   4 dozen

Variations: Add 1 tablespoon sesame seeds.
            Add 2 teaspoons poppy seeds.
            Add 1/4 teaspoon oregano.
            Shape dough into sticks, 1/4-inch in diameter.

To make a basic cream cheese dip, combine an 8-ounce package of softened cream cheese with 1/4 cup of milk and mix until well blended. Use your imagination and add other ingredients like crumbled bacon, diced green pepper, diced shrimp or spices. Chill several hours before serving to blend flavors.

Empanadas Excelentes

1/2 pound ground beef   1 teaspoon chili powder
1/4 cup chopped onion   1/4 teaspoon salt
1 1/2 cups (6 ounces) shredded   1/4 teaspoon Tabasco sauce
  Kraft sharp natural cheddar   Pastry for 2 double crust 9-inch
  cheese   pies
1/4 cup catsup

Brown meat; drain. Add onion; cook until tender. Stir in cheese, catsup and seasonings. Roll pastry to 1/4-inch thickness on lightly floured surface. Cut pastry with 3 1/2-inch round cutter. Spoon about 1 teaspoon meat mixture onto center of each round. Fold in half; press edges together with fork. Bake at 450°, 10 to 12 minutes or until lightly browned. Serve warm.   3 1/2 dozen

Note: Empanadas may be frozen and baked at 450°, 15 minutes. They may be covered, refrigerated and baked at 450°, 12 to 15 minutes or until lightly browned.

Cheddar Appetizer Spritz

3 cups (12 ounces) shredded Kraft   1 3/4 cups flour
   sharp natural cheddar cheese   1/2 teaspoon salt
1/2 cup Parkay margarine   1/8 teaspoon cayenne
2 tablespoons milk

Thoroughly blend cheese, margarine and milk. Add combined dry
ingredients; mix well. Force dough through a cookie press onto
greased cookie sheet. Bake at 375°, 10 to 12 minutes or until edges
are golden brown. 8 dozen

Sunrise Eggs

12 hard-cooked eggs   1/4 cup Kraft real mayonnaise
1 5-ounce jar Kraft pasteurized   1/4 cup milk
   process cheese spread with
   bacon

Cut eggs in half lengthwise. Remove yolks and mash. Blend with
cheese spread, mayonnaise and milk. Fill egg whites.
2 dozen egg halves

Bravo Cheese Spread

2 cups (8 ounces) shredded Casino   2 tablespoons port
   brand natural brick cheese   1/4 teaspoon paprika
2 tablespoons Parkay margarine

Combine all ingredients, mixing until well blended. 1 1/2 cups

---

Basic Spread: An 8-ounce package of softened cream cheese
makes a great spread when it is blended with 2 cups of shredded
sharp cheddar cheese. You can add chopped green pepper and
pimiento, green onion slices or chopped smoked beef.

Sunshine Spread

2 cups (8 ounces) shredded Kraft   1/2 teaspoon dry mustard
   sharp natural cheddar cheese   Dash of cayenne
1 8-ounce package Philadelphia   1 tablespoon chopped chives
   Brand cream cheese   1 teaspoon chopped pimiento
1/4 cup beer

Combine cheddar cheese, softened cream cheese, beer, mustard
and cayenne. Mix until well blended. Stir in chives and pimiento.
1 3/4 cups

Pecan Ball Appetizers

2 8-ounce packages Philadelphia
  Brand cream cheese
2 cups (8 ounces) shredded
  Cracker Barrel brand sharp
  natural cheddar cheese
1 tablespoon chopped pimiento
1 tablespoon chopped green
  pepper

1 tablespoon finely chopped onion
2 teaspoons Worcestershire sauce
1 teaspoon lemon juice
Dash of cayenne
Dash of salt
Chopped pecans, toasted

Combine softened cream cheese and cheddar cheese, mixing until
well blended. Add pimiento, green pepper, onion, Worcestershire
sauce, lemon juice and seasonings; mix well. Chill. Shape into small
balls; roll in nuts.   2 dozen

Variation: Omit pecans and roll balls in chopped fresh parsley.

For a colorful addition to an appetizer tray, spread boiled ham
slices with whipped cream cheese with chives. Roll ham and slice.

Snappy Snack Ball

1 8-ounce package Philadelphia
  Brand cream cheese
1 cup (4 ounces) shredded
  Cracker Barrel brand sharp
  natural cheddar cheese
6 crisply cooked bacon slices,
  crumbled

1 tablespoon chopped green
  pepper
1 teaspoon Worcestershire sauce
1/4 teaspoon onion salt
1/4 teaspoon Tabasco sauce
Chopped fresh parsley

Combine softened cream cheese and cheddar cheese, mixing until
well blended. Stir in bacon, green pepper and seasonings; mix well.
Chill. Shape into a ball; roll in parsley.   1 ball

Lacy Cheese Discs

Kraft midget longhorn style
  natural colby cheese

Cut cheese horizontally into 1/4-inch slices. Turn upright; cut vertically into quarters. Place cheese quarters 2 to 3 inches apart on
Teflon-lined cookie sheet. Bake at 350°, 10 minutes. Remove from
cookie sheet immediately; drain on absorbent paper.

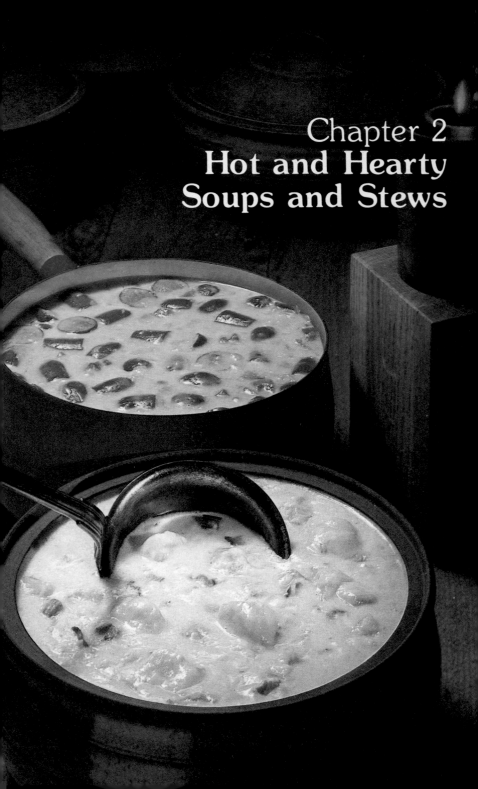

Chapter 2
Hot and Hearty
Soups and Stews

Swiss Potato Potage

1 chicken bouillon cube
1 cup boiling water
3 cups chopped potatoes
1/2 cup chopped celery
1/4 cup chopped onion
1 teaspoon parsley flakes
1 teaspoon salt
Dash of pepper

2 1/2 cups milk
2 tablespoons flour
1 6-ounce package Kraft
   shredded natural Swiss
   cheese
6 crisply cooked bacon slices,
   crumbled

Dissolve bouillon cube in water; add vegetables and seasonings. Cover; simmer 10 minutes or until potatoes are tender. Add a small amount of milk to flour, stirring until well blended. Gradually add flour mixture to hot vegetables. Add remaining milk; cook until mixture boils and thickens. Add cheese and bacon; stir until cheese melts. 6 to 8 servings

Corny Frank Chowder

1 pound frankfurters, sliced
1/2 cup chopped green pepper
1/2 cup chopped onion
2 tablespoons Parkay margarine
1 16-ounce can cream style corn

1 cup milk
3/4 pound Velveeta pasteurized
   process cheese spread, cubed
Dash of pepper

Sauté frankfurters, green pepper and onion in margarine in a 3-quart saucepan. Add remaining ingredients; stir until process cheese spread melts. 6 servings

Potato Parmesan Chowder

3 cups chopped potatoes
1/2 cup chopped onion
2 cups boiling water
1 teaspoon salt
Dash of pepper
2 tablespoons Parkay margarine

2 tablespoons flour
2 cups milk
1 cup (4 ounces) Kraft grated
   parmesan cheese
6 crisply cooked bacon slices,
   crumbled

Combine potatoes, onion, water, salt and pepper. Cover; simmer 15 minutes or until vegetables are tender. Do not drain. Make a white sauce with margarine, flour and milk. Add undrained vegetables. Heat; add cheese and bacon, stirring until cheese is melted. 6 servings

Opposite: Swiss Potato Potage, Corny Frank Chowder

Florentine Soup

1 cup mushroom slices
1/2 cup chopped onion
2 tablespoons Parkay margarine
1 tablespoon flour
1 teaspoon salt
1/4 teaspoon garlic salt
Dash of pepper

3 1/2 cups milk
1 10-ounce package frozen
  chopped spinach, cooked,
  drained
1 8-ounce package Philadelphia
  Brand cream cheese, cubed

Sauté mushrooms and onion in margarine. Blend in flour and seasonings. Gradually add milk; cook, stirring constantly, until mixture boils and thickens. Add remaining ingredients. Stir until cream cheese is melted.   4 to 6 servings

Variation: Soup may also be chilled and served cold.

Sprinkle grated parmesan or romano cheese over the top of soup for added zest. It's particularly good with onion, vegetable, tomato or potato soup.

Laredo Chili

1 pound ground beef
1/2 cup chopped onion
1/2 cup chopped green pepper
1 16-ounce can kidney beans,
  drained

1 cup chopped tomato
1 8-ounce jar Cheez Whiz
  pasteurized process cheese
  spread with jalapeño peppers
2 teaspoons chili powder

Brown meat; drain. Add onion and green pepper; cook until tender. Stir in remaining ingredients; simmer 15 minutes. Serve with corn chips, if desired.   4 to 6 servings

Three Bean Chili

1 16-ounce can pork and beans
1 16-ounce can kidney beans,
  undrained
1 16-ounce can green beans,
  drained

6 crisply cooked bacon slices,
  coarsely crumbled
1 8-ounce jar Cheez Whiz
  pasteurized process cheese
  spread with jalapeño peppers

Combine pork and beans, kidney beans, green beans and bacon; heat. Stir in process cheese spread; continue cooking until hot.
4 to 6 servings

Nob Hill Potato Bisque

2 cups mashed potatoes
2 cups milk
1 8-ounce jar Cheez Whiz
   pasteurized process cheese
   spread

2 tablespoons green onion slices
Dash of pepper

Combine ingredients; heat thoroughly.   4 to 6 servings

Variation: Add 2 tablespoons dry white wine.

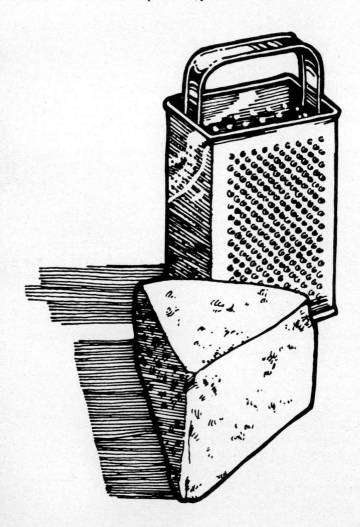

Cookout Stew

4 carrots, quartered
1 1/2 cups chopped potatoes
2 medium onions, quartered
1 10-ounce package frozen peas
 or 1 16-ounce can peas, drained
1/2 pound frankfurters, sliced
 diagonally

1 10 3/4-ounce can condensed
 cream of celery soup
1 8-ounce jar Cheez Whiz
 pasteurized process cheese
 spread

Place carrots, potatoes and onions in a 2-quart saucepan; cover with water. Cover; cook 10 minutes. Add peas and frankfurters. Continue cooking an additional 5 minutes; drain. Stir in soup and process cheese spread; heat. 4 to 6 servings

---

Melt sliced cheddar or muenster cheese on slices of rye bread and serve them as a welcome accompaniment to soup.

Wellington Stew

1 1/2 pounds beef, cut into
 1-inch cubes
1/4 cup Kraft Italian dressing
1 28-ounce can tomatoes
1 teaspoon salt

1/4 teaspoon pepper
2 cups chopped potatoes
1 cup celery slices
12 small whole onions
Cheese Dumplings

Brown meat in dressing. Add tomatoes and seasonings. Cover; simmer 1 hour. Add vegetables; cover and continue simmering until meat and vegetables are tender. Drop dumplings by tablespoonfuls onto hot stew. Cover; simmer 12 to 15 minutes or until dumplings are done. 6 servings

Cheese Dumplings

1 cup all purpose biscuit mix
1/3 cup milk

1 1/2 cups (6 ounces) shredded
 Kraft sharp natural cheddar
 cheese

Combine biscuit mix and milk. Add cheese; mix well.

Cheez Whiz pasteurized process cheese spread makes an excellent base for soup. Heat the Cheez Whiz and then add your favorite ingredients. (This is a wonderful way to use up leftovers.)

Opposite: Cookout Stew

Home-Style Chowder

1 cup chopped potato
1/2 cup carrot slices
1/4 cup green onion slices
1 1/2 cups boiling water
1 8-ounce jar Cheez Whiz
    pasteurized process cheese
    spread

1 10 3/4-ounce can condensed
    cream of celery soup
1 6 1/2-ounce can tuna,
    drained, flaked

Add potato, carrots and onion to water; cover. Simmer 15 minutes or until vegetables are tender. Add process cheese spread and soup; stir until well blended. Add tuna; heat. Garnish with parsley, if desired. 4 servings

Tangy Corn and Tomato Chowder

2 tablespoons Parkay margarine
2 tablespoons flour
1 cup tomato juice
1 16-ounce can tomatoes
1 12-ounce can whole kernel
    corn, drained

1/4 cup (1 ounce) Kraft grated
    parmesan cheese
1/2 teaspoon celery salt
1/4 teaspoon onion powder
Dash of Tabasco sauce

Melt margarine; blend in flour. Gradually add tomato juice. Stir in remaining ingredients; simmer 10 minutes. Sprinkle with additional cheese, if desired. 4 servings

Cheese Fish Chowder

2 cups thin onion slices
2 tablespoons Parkay margarine
2 tablespoons flour
1 1/2 cups water
2 cups chopped potatoes
1 cup celery slices
1 cup carrot slices

1 teaspoon salt
Dash of pepper
1 pound fish fillets, cooked, cut
    into pieces
1 1/2 cups milk
2 cups (8 ounces) shredded Kraft
    sharp natural cheddar cheese

Sauté onion in margarine; blend in flour. Gradually add water; stir in vegetables and seasonings. Cover; simmer 20 minutes or until potatoes are tender. Add remaining ingredients; stir until cheese melts. 8 servings

---

Melt shreds of Swiss cheese on toasted rye rounds. Float them on French onion or tomato soup for added heartiness and flavor.

Dumpling Soup

1/3 cup shredded carrot
1/3 cup celery slices
2 tablespoons green onion slices
1   10 1/2-ounce can condensed
   chicken broth
1 cup milk

1 8-ounce jar Cheez Whiz
   pasteurized process cheese
   spread
1 cup all purpose biscuit mix
2 tablespoons chopped fresh
   parsley

Cook carrot, celery and onion in chicken broth 10 minutes or until tender. Add milk and process cheese spread. Cook over low heat, stirring constantly, until process cheese spread melts. Prepare biscuit mix as directed on package for dumplings, adding parsley. Drop dumplings by teaspoonfuls into simmering soup. Cook over low heat 10 minutes. Cover tightly; continue cooking 10 minutes.
6 servings

Creamy Cheddar Soup

2/3 cup coarsely shredded carrot
2/3 cup thin celery slices
1/4 cup chopped onion
1/4 cup Parkay margarine
1/4 cup flour
1 teaspoon salt

Dash of pepper
4 cups milk
1 cup cooked ham cubes
2 cups (8 ounces) shredded Kraft
   sharp natural cheddar cheese

Sauté vegetables in margarine; blend in flour and seasonings. Gradually add milk; stir in ham. Cook, stirring constantly, until mixture boils and thickens. Add cheese; stir until melted.
4 to 6 servings

American Chowder

1 large onion, sliced
2 tablespoons Parkay margarine
4 cups chopped potatoes
1 cup celery slices
2 cups water
2 teaspoons salt
1/4 teaspoon pepper

2 cups milk
2 tablespoons flour
1 12-ounce package smoked
 sausage links, sliced
1/2 pound Kraft American
 pasteurized process cheese,
 cubed

Sauté onion in margarine. Add potatoes, celery, water and seasonings. Cover; simmer 15 minutes or until vegetables are tender. Add a small amount of milk to flour, stirring until well blended. Gradually add flour mixture to hot vegetables. Add sausage and remaining milk; cook, stirring constantly, until mixture boils and thickens. Add cheese; stir until cheese melts.   8 to 10 servings

Creamy "Philly" Soup

1/3 cup chopped green pepper
1/4 cup chopped onion
2 tablespoons Parkay margarine
1 8-ounce package Philadelphia
 Brand cream cheese, cubed
1 cup milk

1 chicken bouillon cube
1 cup boiling water
1 8 3/4-ounce can cream style
 corn
1/2 teaspoon salt
Dash of pepper

Sauté green pepper and onion in margarine. Add cream cheese and milk. Cook over low heat, stirring until smooth. Dissolve bouillon cube in hot water; stir into cream cheese mixture. Add remaining ingredients. Heat.   4 servings

Hearty Golden Chowder

2 cups chopped potatoes
1/2 cup carrot slices
1/2 cup celery slices
1/4 cup chopped onion
1 tablespoon chopped chives
1 teaspoon salt
Dash of pepper

2 cups boiling water
1/4 cup Parkay margarine
1/4 cup flour
2 cups milk
2 cups (8 ounces) shredded Kraft
 sharp natural cheddar cheese

Add potatoes, carrots, celery, onion, chives, salt and pepper to water. Cover; simmer 10 minutes. Do not drain. Make a white sauce with margarine, flour and milk. Add cheese; stir until melted. Add undrained vegetables. Heat; do not boil. Top with additional chives, if desired.   6 to 8 servings

Beef Stew Borghese

1/2 cups (2 ounces) Kraft
  grated parmesan cheese
3 tablespoons flour
2 pounds beef, cut into 1-inch
  cubes
All purpose oil
1 10 1/2-ounce can condensed
  beef broth
1 16-ounce can tomatoes

1 cup water
3 medium zucchini, sliced
1 8-ounce can small whole
  onions, drained
1 4-ounce can mushrooms, drained

*   *   *

1/4 cup cold water
2 tablespoons flour

Combine 1/4 cup cheese with flour; coat meat. Brown meat in oil; drain. Add broth, tomatoes and water. Cover; simmer 1 hour or until meat is tender. Add remaining vegetables; simmer uncovered 10 minutes.

Combine cold water and flour, stirring until well blended. Gradually add flour mixture to stew; cook, stirring constantly, until mixture boils and thickens. Remove from heat; stir in remaining cheese. 6 to 8 servings

---

Next time you serve stew, offer grated romano or parmesan cheese to sprinkle on top for extra flavor.

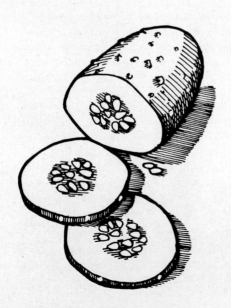

Tuna Cheemato Soup

1 10 3/4-ounce can condensed
   tomato soup
1 1/4 cups water
1 6 1/2-ounce can tuna,
   drained, flaked

1 8-ounce jar Cheez Whiz
   pasteurized process cheese
   spread
Dash of pepper

Combine all ingredients; heat, stirring constantly, until process cheese spread is melted and soup is hot. 4 servings

French Onion Soup

3 cups onion rings
Parkay margarine
4 cups boiling water
4 beef bouillon cubes

Dash of pepper
8 white bread rounds, toasted
Kraft grated parmesan cheese

Sauté onion rings in 2 tablespoons margarine. Add water, bouillon cubes and pepper. Cover; simmer 15 minutes. Spread bread rounds with margarine and top each serving of soup with bread; sprinkle with cheese. 8 servings

Minestrone

1 10 3/4-ounce can condensed
   beef broth
1 16-ounce can tomatoes, chopped
1 tablespoon cornstarch
1 1/4 cups water
1 10-ounce package frozen
   chopped spinach, cooked,
   drained
1 10-ounce package frozen
   Italian green beans, cooked,
   drained

1 cup cooked carrot slices
1 cup large shell macaroni,
   cooked, drained
1/2 cup thin onion slices
1/2 cup (2 ounces) Kraft grated
   parmesan cheese or Kraft
   grated romano cheese
1/8 teaspoon garlic powder

Combine broth, tomatoes and combined cornstarch and water; cook until mixture thickens. Add remaining ingredients; heat. Serve with additional cheese, if desired. 6 servings

---

For a quick and hearty lunch, heat together an 8-ounce jar of Cheez Whiz pasteurized process cheese spread and a 10 3/4-ounce can of tomato soup.

Suburbia Stew

2 pounds beef, cut into 1-inch
   cubes
All purpose oil
1 10 1/2-ounce can condensed
   beef broth
1 cup water
1 bay leaf
2 teaspoons salt

1/4 teaspoon pepper
6 medium onions, quartered
1 1/2 cups celery slices
6 medium carrots, cut into thirds
     *   *   *
1/2 cup (2 ounces) Kraft grated
   parmesan cheese
2 cups hot mashed potatoes

Brown meat in oil; drain. Add broth, water and seasonings. Cover; simmer 1 hour. Add vegetables. Cover; continue simmering 30 minutes or until meat and vegetables are tender. Remove bay leaf. Pour into 10 x 6-inch baking dish.

Stir cheese into potatoes; spoon on top of hot stew. Broil until potatoes are lightly browned. Sprinkle with additional cheese, if desired. 6 to 8 servings

Note: Two 1 1/2-pound cans of canned stew may be used.

Oven Stew

1/3 cup flour
2 teaspoons salt
1/4 teaspoon pepper
2 pounds beef, cut into 1-inch
  cubes
All purpose oil
1/2 cup water

2 cups carrot chunks
1 4-ounce can mushrooms, drained
10 small onions
3 cups hot mashed potatoes
1/2 pound Velveeta pasteurized
  process cheese spread, cubed

Combine flour and seasonings; coat meat. Brown meat in oil; drain.
Combine meat, water, carrots, mushrooms and onions. Pour into
2-quart casserole. Cover; bake at 325°, 2 hours. Combine potatoes
and process cheese spread. Spoon potato mixture around edge of
casserole. Broil until process cheese spread melts.   6 servings

Opposite: Beef Strips Oriental (page 40), Crunchy Parmesan Chicken (page 40)

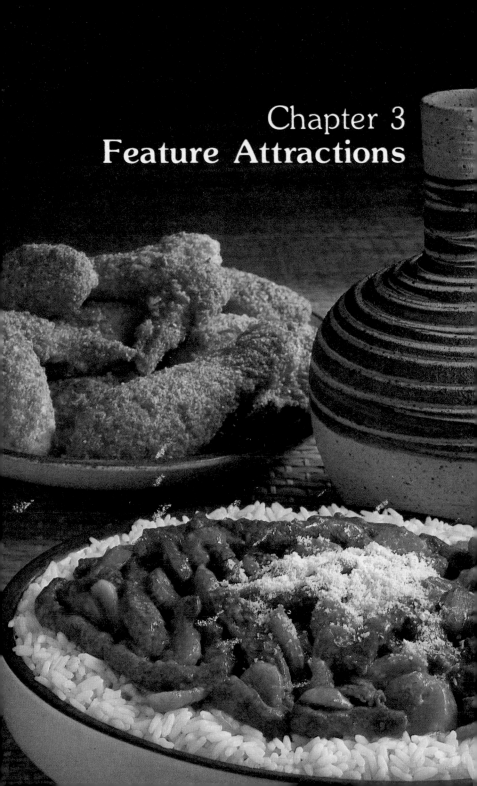

Chapter 3
Feature Attractions

Beef Strips Oriental

1 pound round steak
All purpose oil
1 1/2 cups water
3 tablespoons soy sauce
1 garlic clove, minced
1 cup carrot slices
1 cup celery slices

1 6-ounce can water chestnuts,
    drained, sliced
    *   *   *
1/4 cup cold water
2 tablespoons cornstarch
1/2 cup (2 ounces) Kraft grated
    parmesan cheese
Hot cooked rice

Cut meat into strips 1/4 inch wide and 3 to 4 inches long. Brown meat in oil; drain. Add water, soy sauce and garlic. Cover; simmer 45 minutes. Add vegetables; cover and continue cooking 15 to 20 minutes or until meat and vegetables are tender. Add water chestnuts.

Combine water and cornstarch, stirring until well blended. Gradually add cornstarch mixture to hot meat and vegetables. Cook, stirring constantly, until mixture boils and thickens. Remove from heat; stir in cheese. Serve over rice. Top with additional cheese, if desired.   4 to 6 servings

Crunchy Parmesan Chicken

1 3-ounce can French fried onions,
    crushed
3/4 cup (3 ounces) Kraft grated
    parmesan cheese
1/4 cup dry bread crumbs
1 teaspoon paprika
1/2 teaspoon salt

Dash of pepper
1 2 1/2 to 3-pound broiler-fryer,
    cut up
1 egg, beaten
1 tablespoon milk
1/4 cup Parkay margarine, melted

Combine onion, cheese, crumbs and seasonings. Dip chicken in combined egg and milk; coat with cheese mixture. Place in an 11 3/4 x 7 1/2-inch baking dish. Pour margarine over chicken; bake at 350°, 55 to 60 minutes or until golden brown.   4 servings

Skillet Round-Up

1 16-ounce can pork and beans
1/2 pound frankfurters, cut
    into 1-inch pieces
1/3 cup Kraft barbecue sauce

1 8-ounce jar Cheez Whiz
    pasteurized process cheese
    spread
Corn bread

Combine pork and beans, frankfurters and barbecue sauce; simmer 15 minutes. Stir in process cheese spread; heat. Serve over corn bread.   4 servings

Swiss and Ham Scallop

2 tablespoons Parkay margarine
1/4 cup flour
2 cups milk
1 cup (4 ounces) Kraft shredded
  natural Swiss cheese

3 cups potato slices
2 cups ham cubes
1/2 cup green onion slices

Make a white sauce with margarine, flour and milk. Add cheese; stir until melted. Add remaining ingredients; mix well. Pour into 2-quart casserole; cover and bake at 350°, 1 hour. Uncover; continue baking 30 minutes. 6 servings

Veal alla Parmigiana

1/2 cup flour
Dash of salt and pepper
2 pounds veal cutlets
All purpose oil
1 green pepper, sliced
1 large onion, sliced

1 beef bouillon cube
1 cup boiling water
1 8-ounce can tomato sauce
1/4 cup (1 ounce) Kraft
  grated parmesan cheese
1 bay leaf

Combine flour and seasonings; coat meat. Brown meat on both sides in oil. Add green pepper and onion; cook until tender. Dissolve bouillon cube in water; pour over meat and vegetables. Add remaining ingredients. Cover; simmer 30 minutes. Remove bay leaf. Sprinkle each serving with additional cheese, if desired. 6 servings

Western Strata

8 white bread slices, crusts
  trimmed
Ham slices
4 eggs, beaten
1/2 cup milk
1 8-ounce jar Cheez Whiz
  pasteurized process cheese
  spread

2 tablespoons chopped green
  pepper
1 tablespoon chopped onion
1 tablespoon chopped pimiento
4 green pepper slices

Place four slices of bread on bottom of a greased 8-inch square baking dish. Cover with ham slices. Combine eggs and milk; gradually add to process cheese spread, mixing until well blended. Add green pepper, onion and pimiento. Pour half of mixture over ham. Cover with remaining bread and milk mixture. Top with green pepper rings. Cover; refrigerate 1 hour or overnight. Bake at 350°, 40 minutes. Let stand 10 minutes. Cut into squares. 4 servings

Meatballs Stroganoff

1 pound ground beef
1/3 cup dry bread crumbs
1/3 cup milk
1 egg
1/2 teaspoon Worcestershire
   sauce
1 teaspoon salt
Dash of pepper

1/4 cup all purpose oil
2 tablespoons green onion slices
1 8-ounce package Philadelphia
   Brand cream cheese, cubed
3/4 cup water
1 4-ounce can mushrooms, drained
4 cups (8 ounces) noodles, cooked,
   drained

Combine meat, bread crumbs, milk, egg, Worcestershire sauce and seasonings; mix lightly. Form into 24 meatballs; brown in oil. Cook 10 to 15 minutes or until done; remove meatballs. Drain fat, reserving 1 tablespoon. Add green onion to fat; cook until tender. Add cream cheese, water and mushrooms. Cook over low heat; stir until smooth. Arrange meatballs over hot noodles; cover with sauce.
6 to 8 servings

Toss grated parmesan cheese with bread crumbs and margarine. Sprinkle on top of your favorite casserole for a new taste treat.

Cannelloni

1 pound ground beef
1/4 cup finely chopped
   green pepper
1/4 cup finely chopped onion
1/2 cup dry bread crumbs
1 teaspoon salt
1/4 teaspoon oregano
1 egg, slightly beaten
12 (5 1/2 ounces) cannelloni
   noodles, cooked, drained

1/2 cup (2 ounces) Kraft
   grated parmesan cheese
        *   *   *
1 cup milk
2 8-ounce packages Philadelphia
   Brand cream cheese, cubed
1/2 cup (2 ounces) Kraft
   grated parmesan cheese
1/4 teaspoon salt

Brown meat; drain. Add green pepper and onion; cook until tender. Stir in bread crumbs, seasonings and egg. Fill noodles with meat mixture; place in 11 3/4 x 7 1/2-inch baking dish. Top with parmesan cheese.
   Heat milk and cream cheese over low heat, stirring until smooth. Blend in remaining ingredients. Pour sauce over noodles. Bake at 375°, 20 minutes.   6 servings

Opposite: Meatballs Stroganoff

Azteca Casserole

1 pound ground beef	1 tablespoon chili powder
1/2 cup chopped onion	2 cups corn chips
1/2 cup chopped green pepper	1 8-ounce jar Cheez Whiz
1 12-ounce can whole kernel	pasteurized process cheese
corn	spread or Cheez Whiz
1 cup Kraft barbecue sauce	with jalapeño peppers

Brown meat; drain. Add onion and green pepper; cook until tender. Stir in corn, barbecue sauce and chili powder; heat. Place 1 cup corn chips in bottom of 1 1/2-quart casserole; cover with half of meat mixture and half of process cheese spread. Repeat layers. Bake at 375°, 25 minutes. Garnish with additional corn chips, if desired. 6 servings

Parm-a-Meatloaf

1 1/2 pounds ground beef	1 egg
1 cup soft bread crumbs	1 1/2 teaspoons salt
3/4 cup milk	1/4 teaspoon pepper
1/2 cup chopped onion	1/4 teaspoon oregano
1/2 cup (2 ounces) Kraft	1/3 cup Kraft barbecue sauce
grated parmesan cheese	

Combine all ingredients except barbecue sauce; mix lightly. Shape into loaf in 10 x 6-inch baking dish. Bake at 350°, 45 minutes. Spread with barbecue sauce; continue baking 15 minutes. Serve sprinkled with additional cheese, if desired. 6 servings

Deep Dish Meat Pie

1 pound ground beef	2 tablespoons Parkay margarine
1/4 cup chopped onion	2 tablespoons flour
1 10-ounce package frozen peas	1/2 teaspoon salt
and carrots, cooked, drained	1 cup water
1 cup chopped cooked potato	1 8-ounce can refrigerated
1/2 pound Velveeta	crescent dinner rolls
pasteurized process cheese	
spread, cubed	

Brown meat; drain. Add onion; cook until tender. Combine meat mixture, peas and carrots, potatoes and process cheese spread; mix well. Pour into 11 3/4 x 7 1/2-inch baking dish. Melt margarine in saucepan over low heat. Blend in flour and salt. Gradually add water; cook, stirring constantly, until thickened. Pour over meat mixture. Unroll both halves of refrigerated dough into flat rectangular sheets. Fit to cover baking dish. Bake at 375°, 20 to 25 minutes or until golden brown. 6 to 8 servings

Mozzarella Meat Pie

1 pound ground beef
1/3 cup chopped onion
1/3 cup chopped celery
1 6-ounce can tomato paste
1 4-ounce package Kraft
shredded natural low
moisture part-skim
mozzarella cheese

1/2 teaspoon oregano
1/2 teaspoon salt
Dash of pepper
1 8-ounce can refrigerated
crescent dinner rolls

Brown meat; drain. Add onion and celery; cook until tender. Add tomato paste, 1/2 cup cheese and seasonings; mix well. Separate crescent dough into eight triangles. Place in 9-inch pie plate, pressing together to form crust. Flute edge. Fill with meat mixture; top with remaining cheese. Bake at 375°, 15 to 20 minutes or until crust is golden brown. 6 to 8 servings

Swiss Meatloaf

1 8-ounce package Kraft
natural Swiss cheese slices
2 pounds ground beef
1 1/2 cups soft bread crumbs
1/3 cup Kraft barbecue sauce
1/2 cup milk

1/2 cup chopped onion
1/2 cup chopped green pepper
1 egg
1 1/2 teaspoons salt
1/4 teaspoon pepper

Cut 2 cheese slices into triangles. Chop remaining cheese. Combine remaining ingredients; mix lightly. Shape into loaf in 11 3/4 x 7 1/2-inch baking dish. Bake at 350°, 1 1/2 hours. Arrange triangles of cheese on loaf; continue baking until cheese melts.
6 to 8 servings

Cheddar Meatloaf

1 1/2 pounds ground beef
1 1/4 cups dry bread crumbs
1 4-ounce package Kraft
shredded sharp natural
cheddar cheese
1 10 3/4-ounce can condensed
tomato soup

1 egg
1/4 cup chopped onion
2 tablespoons chopped, fresh
parsley
1/2 teaspoon salt
Dash of pepper

Combine all ingredients; mix lightly. Shape into loaf in 11 3/4 x 7 1/2-inch baking dish. Bake at 350°, 1 hour. 6 servings

Stir a cup of shredded Swiss cheese into 2 cups of medium white sauce. Add the cheese sauce to hot cooked macaroni and you'll have a simple main dish with a special flavor.

Ground Beef Grand Style

1 1/2 pounds ground beef
1 cup chopped onion
1 8-ounce package Philadelphia
   Brand cream cheese
1 10 3/4-ounce can condensed
   cream of mushroom soup

1 teaspoon salt
1/4 cup catsup
1 8-ounce can refrigerated
   buttermilk biscuits

Brown meat; drain. Add onion; cook until tender. Add cream cheese and soup; stir until smooth. Add salt and catsup; pour into 2-quart casserole. Top with biscuits. Bake at 375°, 25 minutes or until golden brown.   6 to 8 servings

Homesteader's Casserole

1 9-ounce package frozen cut
   green beans, cooked, drained
1 8-ounce can small whole
   onions, drained
1 tablespoon chopped pimiento

3 cups hot mashed potatoes
1 pound pork sausage links,
   cooked, drained
1/2 pound Velveeta pasteurized
   process cheese spread, sliced

Combine green beans, onions and pimiento. Layer half the potatoes, sausage and process cheese spread in a 2-quart casserole. Top with remaining potatoes, combined vegetables, remaining sausage and process cheese spread. Cover; bake at 350°, 30 minutes.   4 to 6 servings

Oriental Casserole

2 tablespoons Parkay margarine
2 tablespoons flour
1 1/2 cups milk
1 teaspoon soy sauce
1/2 teaspoon salt
1/4 teaspoon pepper
2 cups (8 ounces) shredded Kraft
   sharp natural cheddar cheese

2 cups cooked rice
2 cups chopped cooked chicken
1 8 1/2-ounce can water
   chestnuts, drained, sliced
1 2 1/2-ounce jar mushrooms,
   drained
1 3-ounce can chow mein noodles

Make a white sauce with margarine, flour, milk and seasonings. Add cheese; stir until melted. Combine rice, chicken, water chestnuts and mushrooms. Layer half of rice mixture and cheese sauce in 2-quart casserole; repeat layers. Place noodles around edge of casserole. Bake at 350°, 25 minutes.   6 to 8 servings

---

Sprinkle grated parmesan or romano cheese on toasted English muffins to provide a zesty base for chicken à la king and other creamed dishes.

Seacoast Casserole

1/4 cup Parkay margarine
1/4 cup flour
2 1/2 cups milk
1 teaspoon salt
Dash of pepper
1 1/2 cups (6 ounces) shredded
  Kraft sharp natural cheddar
  cheese

1/4 cup (1 ounce) Kraft
  grated parmesan cheese
1 pound fish fillets, cooked, flaked
1 2 1/2-ounce jar mushrooms,
  drained
1/4 cup chopped pimiento
Hot cooked rice

Make a white sauce with margarine, flour, milk and seasonings. Add cheddar cheese and parmesan cheese; stir until melted. Stir in fish, mushrooms and pimiento; heat. Serve over rice. Garnish with parsley, if desired.   6 servings

Wagon Wheel Casserole

3 cups hot cooked rice
1 8-ounce jar Cheez Whiz
  pasteurized process cheese
  spread
1/4 cup chopped fresh parsley

1/4 cup chopped pitted
  ripe olives
8 boiled ham slices
1/2 cup Kraft barbecue sauce

Combine rice, process cheese spread, parsley and olives; mix lightly. Pour into 2-quart casserole. Spread ham slices with 1/4 cup barbecue sauce; roll up, starting at narrow end. Arrange on top of rice mixture; spoon remaining barbecue sauce over ham rolls. Bake at 350°, 20 minutes. Garnish with additional parsley and olives, if desired.   4 servings

Harvest Casserole

1 package Kraft tangy Italian
  style spaghetti dinner
1/2 cup chopped green pepper
2 tablespoons Parkay margarine
1 16-ounce can tomatoes

1/2 cup water
1 1/2 cup chopped cooked chicken
Velveeta pasteurized process
  cheese spread

Cook spaghetti; drain. Sauté green pepper in margarine. Stir in tomatoes, water, The Herb Spice Mix and The Grated Parmesan Cheese. Add spaghetti, chicken and 1/2 pound process cheese spread, cubed; mix well. Pour into 2-quart casserole. Bake at 350°, 25 minutes. Top with additional process cheese spread slices; continue baking until process cheese spread melts.   6 to 8 servings

Variation: Casserole may be covered and refrigerated overnight. Bake at 350°, 40 minutes.

Napoli Casserole

2 tablespoons Parkay margarine
2 tablespoons flour
1 cup milk
1/2 teaspoon salt
1 cup (4 ounces) Kraft shredded
  natural low moisture part-
  skim mozzarella cheese

1/2 pound mild Italian sausage
1 medium zucchini, sliced
1/4 cup chopped onion
2 cups (4 ounces) noodles,
  cooked, drained
1/2 cup chopped tomato

Make a white sauce with margarine, flour, milk and salt. Add 1/2 cup cheese; stir until melted. Remove sausage from casing; cut into pieces. Brown in skillet. Add zucchini and onion. Cook until tender; drain. Stir in sauce, noodles and tomato. Pour into 1-quart casserole. Top with remaining cheese; bake at 350°, 20 minutes.
4 servings

Everyday Cheddar Casserole

1/4 cup Parkay margarine
1/4 cup flour
2 cups milk
1 teaspoon salt
Dash of cayenne
2 cups (8 ounces) shredded Kraft
  sharp natural cheddar cheese

2 cups (7 ounces) elbow
  macaroni, cooked, drained
1/2 pound frankfurters, sliced
1 10-ounce package frozen peas
  and carrots, cooked, drained

Make a white sauce with margarine, flour, milk and seasonings. Add cheese; stir until melted. Stir in remaining ingredients. Pour into 1 1/2-quart casserole bake at 350°, 20 minutes.   6 servings

Quick Change Combo

2 cups (7 ounces) elbow
  macaroni, cooked, drained
1 8-ounce jar Cheez Whiz
  pasteurized process cheese
  spread
1 12-ounce can luncheon meat,
  cut into strips

1 cup chopped celery
3/4 cup Kraft barbecue sauce
1/4 cup Kraft real mayonnaise
2 cups bread cubes
3 tablespoons Parkay margarine,
  melted

Combine hot macaroni and process cheese spread. Add meat, celery, barbecue sauce and mayonnaise; mix well. Pour into 2-quart casserole. Top with bread cubes tossed with margarine. Bake at 350°, 50 minutes.   6 to 8 servings

Variation: To make a cold main dish, omit bread cubes and margarine and do not bake. Chill and serve in a lettuce lined bowl.

Hurry-Up Ham Supper

1/2 cup chopped green pepper
1/4 cup Parkay margarine
1/4 cup flour
1 teaspoon salt
Dash of cayenne
2 cups milk
2 cups (8 ounces) shredded
  Kraft sharp natural
  cheddar cheese

2 cups (7 ounces) elbow
  macaroni, cooked, drained
1 cup ham cubes
6 tomato slices

Sauté green pepper in margarine; blend in flour and seasonings. Gradually add milk; cook, stirring constantly, until thickened. Add 1 1/2 cups cheese; stir until melted. Stir in macaroni and ham; pour into 1 1/2-quart casserole. Top with tomatoes; bake at 350°, 20 minutes. Top with remaining cheese; continue baking until cheese melts.   6 servings

Tuna Noodle Supper

1 8-ounce jar Cheez Whiz
  pasteurized process cheese
  spread
1 10-ounce package frozen
  peas, cooked, drained
1 6 1/2-ounce can tuna,
  drained, flaked

2 cups (4 ounces) noodles,
  cooked, drained
1 2 1/2-ounce jar mushrooms,
  drained

Heat process cheese spread over low heat; stir until smooth. Add remaining ingredients; heat.   4 servings

Crusty Fish Fillets

1/2 cup (2 ounces) Kraft
  grated parmesan cheese
1/2 cup yellow cornmeal
1 1/2 teaspoons salt

2 pounds fish fillets
1/2 cup milk
Squeeze Parkay margarine

Combine cheese, cornmeal and salt. Dip fish in milk; coat with cornmeal mixture. Fry on both sides in margarine until fish is browned and flakes easily with a fork.   6 servings

---

Top cooked meat loaf with thin slices of Swiss or cheddar cheese to add variety to meals. Place in a 350° oven, just long enough to melt cheese immediately before serving.

Mission Seafood Bake

1/4 cup Parkay margarine
1/4 cup flour
1 1/2 cups milk
1/2 teaspoon salt
1 1/2 cups (6 ounces) shredded
    Casino brand natural
    monterey jack cheese

2 cups cooked rice
1 6-ounce package frozen
    cooked crabmeat, thawed
1/3 cup slivered almonds, toasted
1/3 cup green onion slices
1 tablespoon sherry

Make a white sauce with margarine, flour, milk and salt. Add 1 cup cheese; stir until melted. Add rice, crabmeat, nuts, onion and sherry; mix well. Pour into 1 1/2-quart casserole. Bake at 350°, 40 minutes. Top with remaining cheese; continue baking until cheese is melted.   6 to 8 servings

Variation: 1 cup of finely chopped ham may be substituted for crabmeat.

Creole Fish Fillets

1/2 cup chopped celery
1/4 cup chopped onion
1/4 cup chopped green pepper
2 tablespoons Parkay margarine
2 tablespoons flour

1 cup chopped tomato
1/2 pound Velveeta pasteurized
    process cheese spread, cubed
4 to 6 fish fillets, broiled

Sauté celery, onion and green pepper in margarine. Blend in flour. Stir in tomato and process cheese spread. Cook, stirring constantly, until process cheese spread melts and mixture thickens. Serve over hot broiled fish.   4 to 6 servings

Fish 'n Macaroni and Cheese

1/4 cup Parkay margarine
1/4 cup flour
2 cups milk
1 1/2 teaspoons salt
Dash of pepper

2 cups (8 ounces) shredded Kraft
    sharp natural cheddar cheese
2 cups (7 ounces) elbow
    macaroni, cooked, drained
8 4-inch frozen fish sticks

Make a white sauce with margarine, flour, milk and seasonings. Add cheese; stir until melted. Stir in macaroni. Pour into a greased 8-inch square baking dish. Top with fish. Bake at 350°, 20 to 25 minutes or until hot.   8 servings

Dress up your favorite macaroni casserole by melting slices of Velveeta pasteurized process cheese spread on top. The melted process cheese spread will enhance the appearance and flavor.

Tuna-Noodle Crispy

1/2 pound Velveeta pasteurized
   process cheese spread, cubed
1 10 3/4-ounce can condensed
   cream of mushroom soup
1/2 cup milk
2 cups (4 ounces) noodles,
   cooked, drained

1 6 1/2-ounce can tuna,
   drained, flaked
Dash of pepper
1/2 cup coarsely crumbled
   crackers
2 tablespoons Parkay margarine,
   melted

Heat process cheese spread, soup and milk over low heat. Stir until sauce is smooth. Add noodles, tuna and pepper; mix well. Pour into 2-quart casserole; top with crackers tossed with margarine. Bake at 325°, 20 minutes. 4 to 6 servings

Tuna Tetrazzini

4 ounces spaghetti, cooked,
   drained
1 10 3/4-ounce can condensed
   cream of celery soup
1/2 cup milk
2 6 1/2-ounce cans tuna,
   drained, flaked

1 4-ounce can mushrooms,
   undrained
1/3 cup chopped onion
1/4 cup pitted ripe olive slices
2 cups (8 ounces) shredded Kraft
   sharp natural cheddar cheese

Combine all ingredients except 1/2 cup cheese; mix lightly. Pour into 1 1/2-quart casserole; bake at 350°, 45 minutes. Top with remaining cheese; continue baking until cheese melts.
6 to 8 servings

Chicken Pie

1 cup chopped potato
1 10-ounce package frozen
   peas and carrots
1 cup boiling water
1/4 cup chopped onion
2 tablespoons Parkay margarine
2 tablespoons flour

1 teaspoon salt
1 cup milk
Velveeta pasteurized
   process cheese spread
2 cups chopped cooked chicken
Pastry for 9-inch pie crust

Add potato and peas and carrots to water. Simmer 10 minutes; drain. Sauté onion in margarine. Blend in flour and salt. Gradually add milk; cook, stirring constantly, until thickened. Add 1/2 pound process cheese spread, cubed; stir until melted. Stir in vegetables and chicken. Spoon mixture into 1 1/2-quart casserole. Roll pastry dough into 7-inch circle. Divide into sixths. Place over chicken mixture. Bake at 400°, 25 minutes. Top with process cheese spread slices; continue baking until melted. 6 servings

Chicken Scampi

1 2 1/2 to 3-pound broiler-fryer,
  cut up
1/4 cup Parkay margarine
2 medium onions, sliced
1 8-ounce can tomato sauce
1/4 cup chopped fresh parsley
1 teaspoon salt
1/2 teaspoon oregano

1/4 teaspoon garlic powder
Dash of pepper
1 cup (5 ounces) cleaned
  cooked shrimp
1/2 cup (2 ounces) Kraft
  grated parmesan cheese
1/2 cup dry red wine
Hot cooked rice

Brown chicken on all sides in margarine. Add onion; cook until
tender. Stir in tomato sauce, parsley and seasonings. Cover;
simmer 45 minutes or until chicken is tender. Stir in shrimp, cheese
and wine; heat. Serve over rice.   4 to 6 servings

Chicken 'n Rice Bake

1 1/2 cups cooked rice
1 8-ounce jar Cheez Whiz
  pasteurized process cheese
  spread
2 cups chopped cooked chicken

1 10-ounce package frozen
  peas, cooked, drained
1 3 1/2-ounce can French fried
  onions

Combine rice and process cheese spread, mixing until well blended.
Stir in chicken and peas. Pour into 10 x 6-inch baking dish. Bake at
350°, 15 minutes. Top with onions; continue baking 5 to 10 minutes
or until hot.   4 to 6 servings

Chicken à la Cheddar

1 10-ounce package Cracker
  Barrel brand sharp
  natural cheddar cheese
2 1/2 pounds (4) whole chicken
  breasts, boned, skinned
2 eggs, beaten
3/4 cup dry bread crumbs
Parkay margarine
1/2 cup chopped onion
1/2 cup chopped green pepper
2 tablespoons flour
1 teaspoon salt

1/4 teaspoon pepper
3/4 cup water
2 cups cooked rice
1 cup cooked wild rice
*   *   *
1 1/2 cups mushroom slices
1/4 cup Parkay margarine
3 tablespoons flour
1 chicken bouillon cube
1/2 cup boiling water
1/2 cup milk
1/3 cup dry white wine

Cut cheese into 8 equal sticks. Cut chicken breasts in half; flatten each half to 1/4-inch thickness. Roll each piece of chicken around a stick of cheese; secure with wooden picks. Dip in eggs, then in bread crumbs. Brown in margarine. Sauté onion and green pepper in 1/4 cup margarine; blend in flour and seasonings. Gradually add water; cook, stirring constantly, until thickened. Stir in rice; pour into 11 3/4 x 7 1/2-inch baking dish. Top with chicken; bake at 400°, 20 minutes.

Sauté mushrooms in margarine; blend in flour. Dissolve bouillon cube in water; gradually add to mushroom mixture. Stir in milk; cook, stirring constantly, until thickened. Add wine; heat. Serve over chicken.   8 servings

Surprise Chicken and Stuffing

1 8-ounce package herb
  seasoned stuffing
1 cup chopped apple
1/2 cup chopped onion
3/4 cup (3 ounces) Kraft
  grated parmesan cheese

1/4 cup Parkay margarine
1 1/2 cups boiling water
*   *   *
1 3 to 3 1/2-pound roasting
  chicken, washed and dried
Parkay margarine, melted

Combine stuffing, apple, onion and cheese. Melt margarine in water. Add to stuffing mixture, stirring until well blended.

Fill neck area of chicken with stuffing. Fasten neck skin to back with skewer. Fold wings across back of chicken, tips touching. Fill body cavity lightly, using about 1 to 1 1/2 cups stuffing. Tie drumsticks to tail. Place chicken, breast side up, in 11 3/4 x 7 1/2-inch baking dish. Brush with margarine. Bake at 375°, 1 1/2 hours. Place remaining stuffing in baking dish surrounding chicken; continue baking 30 minutes.   6 servings

Variation: Bake stuffing in an 8-inch square pan at 350°, 30 minutes.

Homespun Meat Pie

1 pound ground beef
1 4-ounce can mushrooms, drained
1 egg
1/3 cup chopped onion
1/4 cup dry bread crumbs
1 teaspoon salt
Dash of pepper

2 cups chopped potatoes, cooked
3 tablespoons milk
1/2 pound Velveeta
  pasteurized process cheese
  spread, cubed
1 tablespoon chopped fresh parsley
1/4 teaspoon salt

*   *   *

Combine meat, mushrooms, egg, onion, bread crumbs and seasonings; mix lightly. Press meat mixture onto bottom and sides of 9-inch pie plate. Bake at 400°, 15 minutes. Remove meat shell from oven; reduce oven temperature to 350°. Drain excess fat from meat shell.

Mash hot potatoes with milk; stir in process cheese spread, parsley and salt. Fill hot meat shell with potato mixture. Return to oven; continue baking 10 minutes.   6 servings

Homestead Macaroni

6 crisply cooked bacon slices
2 cups (7 ounces) elbow
  macaroni, cooked, drained
1 8-ounce jar Cheez Whiz
  pasteurized process cheese
  spread

Paprika

Crumble four slices bacon. Combine hot macaroni, process cheese spread and crumbled bacon; heat. Sprinkle with paprika. Top with remaining bacon.   4 to 6 servings

Fettuccine

1/2 cup Parkay margarine
1/4 teaspoon garlic salt
4 cups (8 ounces) noodles,
  cooked, drained

3/4 cup (3 ounces) Kraft
  grated parmesan cheese

Melt margarine; stir in garlic salt. Combine hot noodles, cheese and seasoned margarine; toss lightly.   4 servings

Opposite: Homespun Meat Pie

Italian Spaghetti Pie

7 ounces spaghetti, cooked,
  drained
2 eggs, beaten
1/4 cup (1 ounce) Kraft grated
  parmesan cheese
2 tablespoons parsley flakes
1 8-ounce package Kraft shredded
  natural low moisture part-
  skim mozzarella cheese

1 6-ounce can tomato paste
1 cup water
1 4-ounce can mushrooms, drained
1 tablespoon Parkay margarine
1/2 teaspoon celery salt
1/2 teaspoon oregano
1/2 teaspoon garlic salt
1/4 teaspoon salt

Combine spaghetti, eggs, parmesan cheese and parsley. In a greased 9-inch pie plate, layer half the spaghetti mixture and mozzarella
cheese; repeat layers. Bake at 350°, 12 minutes. Combine tomato
paste, water, mushrooms, margarine and seasonings; simmer 10
minutes. Cut pie into wedges and serve with hot sauce.
6 servings

Three Cheese Spaghetti

1 tablespoon Parkay margarine
1 tablespoon flour
1 cup milk
1/4 teaspoon salt
1/2 cup (2 ounces) shredded
  Kraft natural Swiss cheese
1/2 cup (2 ounces) shredded
  Kraft baby gouda cheese
1 2 1/2-ounce jar mushrooms,
  drained

*   *   *

7 ounces spaghetti, cooked,
  drained
2 tablespoons Parkay margarine,
  melted
1 tablespoon chopped fresh parsley
1/2 cup (2 ounces) Kraft grated
  parmesan cheese

Make a white sauce with margarine, flour, milk and salt. Add Swiss
cheese and gouda cheese; stir until melted. Add mushrooms; heat.
   Toss hot spaghetti with margarine, parsley and parmesan
cheese. Pour hot cheese sauce over spaghetti. Serve immediately.
6 to 8 servings

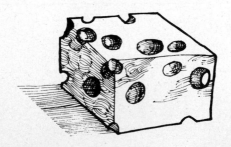

Zesty Italian Supper

1 pound ground beef
　or bulk pork sausage
1/2 cup chopped onion
1/2 cup chopped green pepper
1 8-ounce can tomato sauce
1 4-ounce can mushrooms,
　drained

1/2 teaspoon oregano
1 8-ounce jar Cheez Whiz
　pasteurized process cheese
　spread
Hot cooked mostaccioli noodles
　or spaghetti

Brown meat; drain. Add onion and green pepper; cook until tender. Add tomato sauce, mushrooms and oregano. Cover; simmer 20 minutes. Stir in process cheese spread; heat. Serve over mostaccioli.　4 to 6 servings

Roman Mostaccioli

1 pound ground beef
1/2 cup chopped green pepper
1/2 cup chopped onion
1 16-ounce can tomatoes
1 6-ounce can tomato paste
3/4 cup water
1 bay leaf

1 teaspoon salt
1/4 teaspoon oregano
1/4 teaspoon pepper
2 cups (4 ounces) mostaccioli
　noodles, cooked, drained
1/2 cup (2 ounces) Kraft
　grated romano cheese

Brown meat; drain. Add green pepper and onion; cook until tender. Stir in tomatoes, tomato paste, water and seasonings; simmer 15 minutes. Stir in noodles and cheese; continue cooking an additional 5 minutes. Remove bay leaf. Sprinkle with additional cheese, if desired.　6 servings

Quick-Mix Pizza

1 cup flour
1 teaspoon salt
1/2 teaspoon oregano
2 eggs
2/3 cup milk
1 pound mild Italian sausage
1/4 cup chopped onion

1 4-ounce can mushrooms,
　drained
1 8-ounce can tomato sauce
1 8-ounce package Kraft shredded
　natural low moisture part-
　skim mozzarella cheese

Combine flour, salt, 1/4 teaspoon oregano, eggs and milk; mix until smooth. Pour into well greased and floured 14-inch pizza pan. Remove sausage from casing; cut into pieces. Brown in skillet; drain. Top batter with meat, onion and mushrooms. Bake at 425°, 25 minutes. Combine tomato sauce and remaining 1/4 teaspoon oregano. Pour over pizza; top with cheese. Continue baking 10 minutes.　6 to 8 servings

Zucchini Luncheon Omelet

3 bacon slices
1 medium zucchini, sliced
1 small onion, sliced
2 tablespoons Parkay margarine
6 eggs, beaten
1/3 cup milk

1/2 teaspoon salt
Dash of pepper
1 cup (4 ounces) shredded
    Cracker Barrel brand sharp
    natural cheddar cheese

Fry bacon until crisp; remove from skillet. Drain fat, reserving 1 tablespoon. Cook zucchini and onion in bacon fat until tender. Melt margarine in 10-inch skillet over low heat. Combine eggs, milk and seasonings; pour into skillet. Cook slowly. As egg mixture sets, lift slightly with a spatula to allow uncooked portion to flow underneath. When set, cover omelet with 3/4 cup cheese, zucchini, onion and crumbled bacon. Fold in half; sprinkle with remaining cheese.
3 to 4 servings

Golden Cheddar Omelet

1/2 cup mushroom slices
2 tablespoons green onion slices
    or chopped green pepper
3 tablespoons Parkay margarine
6 eggs, beaten

1/3 cup milk
1/2 teaspoon salt
Dash of pepper
1 cup (4 ounces) shredded Kraft
    sharp natural cheddar cheese

Sauté mushrooms and onion in margarine in a 10-inch skillet. Remove vegetables from skillet. Combine eggs, milk and seasonings; pour into skillet. Cook slowly. As egg mixture sets, lift slightly with a spatula to allow uncooked portion to flow underneath. When set, cover omelet with mushrooms, onion and 3/4 cup cheese. Fold in half; sprinkle with remaining cheese.
3 to 4 servings

Denver Omelet

1/4 cup chopped green pepper
1 tablespoon chopped onion
3 tablespoons Parkay margarine
6 eggs, beaten
1/2 cup chopped ham

1/3 cup milk
Salt and pepper
1/4 pound Velveeta pasteurized
    process cheese spread, sliced,
    cut in half diagonally

Sauté green pepper and onion in margarine in 10-inch skillet. Combine eggs, meat, milk and seasonings; pour into skillet. Cook slowly. As egg mixture sets, lift slightly with a spatula to allow uncooked portion to flow underneath. When set, fold in half. Top with process cheese spread.   3 to 4 servings

Beef and Noodles Midwestern

1 pound ground beef
1/2 cup chopped onion
2 cups (4 ounces) noodles,
  cooked, drained
1 8-ounce jar Cheez Whiz
  pasteurized process cheese
  spread

1 2 1/2-ounce jar mushrooms,
  drained
1/2 teaspoon salt
1/4 teaspoon pepper
1/4 teaspoon paprika

Brown meat; drain. Add onion; cook until tender. Stir in noodles, process cheese spread, mushrooms and seasonings. Heat.
4 servings

Turkey Noodle Bake

1 cup celery slices
1/2 cup chopped onion
Parkay margarine
1/4 cup milk
Velveeta pasteurized process
  cheese spread

1 1/2 cups chopped cooked turkey
2 tablespoons chopped pimiento
2 cups (4 ounces) noodles,
  cooked, drained
1/4 cup dry bread crumbs

Sauté celery and onion in 1 tablespoon margarine. Stir in milk and 1/2 pound process cheese spread, cubed. Cook over low heat; stir until sauce is smooth. Add turkey and pimiento; mix well. Layer noodles and turkey mixture in 10 x 6-inch baking dish. Top with crumbs tossed with 2 tablespoons melted margarine. Bake at 350°, 25 minutes. Top with process cheese spread slices, cut into triangles; continue baking until process cheese spread melts.
6 servings

Enchiladas Olé

1/4 cup finely chopped onion
1/4 cup Parkay margarine
1 8-ounce can tomato sauce
1/4 cup finely chopped green
  chili peppers

1 8-ounce jar Cheez Whiz
  pasteurized process cheese
  spread or Cheez Whiz
  with jalapeño peppers
6 tortillas
All purpose oil
1 16-ounce can refried beans

Sauté onion in margarine. Add tomato sauce and chili peppers; simmer 15 minutes. Stir in process cheese spread; heat. Dip each tortilla in hot oil to soften. Spread tortillas with beans; roll up and place seam side down in a 10 x 6-inch baking dish. Cover with tomato sauce mixture. Bake at 350°, 25 minutes. 6 servings

Enchiladas Aztecas

2 tablespoons Parkay margarine
2 tablespoons flour
1 cup milk
1 teaspoon salt
3 cups (12 ounces) shredded
  Casino brand natural
  monterey jack cheese
2 cups chopped cooked chicken

1/2 cup chopped avocado
1/3 cup chopped tomato
1/3 cup pitted ripe olive slices
1/4 cup chopped green chili
  peppers
1/4 cup chopped onion
12 tortillas
All purpose oil

Make a white sauce with margarine, flour, milk and salt. Add 2 cups cheese; stir until melted. Add chicken, avocado, tomato, olives, chili peppers and onion; mix well. Dip each tortilla in hot oil to soften. Place about 1/3 cup chicken mixture on each tortilla; roll up tightly. Place seam side down in 11 3/4 x 7 1/2-inch baking dish. Top with remaining cheese. Bake at 350°, 20 to 25 minutes or until hot.
6 to 8 servings

Cheesy Chili Enchiladas

3 cups (12 ounces) shredded
  Kraft sharp natural cheddar
  cheese
2 tablespoons flour
1/2 cup chopped onion
2 tablespoons Parkay margarine
1/2 pound ground beef
2 8-ounce cans tomato sauce

1 16-ounce can kidney beans,
  undrained
1 tablespoon chili powder
1/2 teaspoon salt
Dash of Tabasco sauce
12 tortillas
All purpose oil

Toss together 2 1/2 cups cheese and flour. Sauté onion in margarine. Remove from heat; stir in cheese mixture. Brown meat; drain. Add tomato sauce, kidney beans and seasonings; simmer 10 minutes. Dip each tortilla in hot oil to soften. Place approximately 1/4 cup cheese mixture on each tortilla; roll up tightly. Place seam side down in an 11 3/4 x 7 1/2-inch baking dish. Cover with meat mixture. Cover dish with aluminum foil; bake at 350°, 20 to 25 minutes or until hot. Top with remaining cheese.
6 to 8 servings

Taco Stackups

8 tortillas
All purpose oil
1 pound ground beef
3/4 cup Kraft barbecue sauce
1/2 cup water
2 tablespoons chopped green
   chili pepper
1 tablespoon chili powder

Bean dip
Shredded lettuce
Chopped tomato
Chopped avocado
Chopped onion
Dairy sour cream
2 cups (8 ounces) shredded Kraft
   sharp natural cheddar cheese

Fry tortillas in 1/4 inch of hot oil, turning once; drain. Brown meat; drain. Add barbecue sauce, water, chili pepper and chili powder. Simmer 15 minutes, stirring occasionally. For each serving, spread tortilla with bean dip. Top with lettuce, meat mixture, tomato, avocado, onion, sour cream and 1/4 cup cheese. Sprinkle with taco sauce, if desired.   8 servings

Macaroni and Cheese Supreme

2 cups (8 ounces) shredded Kraft
   sharp natural cheddar cheese
1 cup milk
2 eggs, beaten
1/4 cup Parkay margarine, melted

1 teaspoon salt
2 cups (7 ounces) elbow
   macaroni, cooked, drained
Tomato slices
Kraft grated parmesan cheese

Combine cheddar cheese, milk, eggs, margarine and salt; stir in macaroni. Pour into greased 8-inch square baking dish or into 1 1/2-quart casserole. Bake at 425°, 20 minutes. Top with tomatoes and parmesan cheese. Continue baking 10 minutes or until set. 4 to 6 servings

Ham Cheese Strata

8 white bread slices, crusts
   trimmed
1 8-ounce package Deluxe
   Choice sharp • Old English
   pasteurized process cheese
1 cup chopped ham

4 eggs, beaten
2 cups milk
1/2 teaspoon salt
1/4 teaspoon dry mustard
Dash of pepper

Place four slices of bread on bottom of greased 8-inch square baking dish. Cover with four cheese slices, ham, remaining cheese slices and remaining bread slices. Combine eggs, milk and seasonings; pour over bread. Cover; refrigerate 1 hour or overnight. Bake at 325°, 1 hour. Let stand 10 minutes and cut into squares.   4 servings

Swiss Cheese Strata

9 white bread slices, crusts   4 eggs, beaten
  trimmed   2 cups milk
1 6-ounce package Kraft shredded   2 teaspoons prepared mustard
  natural Swiss cheese   1 teaspoon salt

Cut slices of bread into quarters and place half the bread in 11 3/4 x
7 1/2-inch baking dish. Sprinkle cheese over bread. Top with
remaining bread. Combine eggs, milk, mustard and salt; pour over
bread. Bake at 300°, 45 to 50 minutes or until set.
4 to 6 servings

Range Rider's Round Steak

2 pounds round steak   1/4 cup water
3 tablespoons Parkay margarine   1 8-ounce jar Cheez Whiz
1 cup green pepper slices   pasteurized process cheese
1 cup onion slices   spread
1 6-ounce can tomato paste

Cut meat into serving size pieces. In a large skillet, brown meat in
margarine. Add green pepper and onion. Cook until vegetables are
tender; drain. Combine tomato paste with water; pour over meat
and vegetables. Cover; simmer 45 to 50 minutes or until meat is
tender. Add process cheese spread; continue cooking until process
cheese spread melts.   4 to 6 servings

Simple Country Supper

1 pound ground beef   1/2 pound Velveeta pasteurized
1 cup chopped onion   process cheese spread, cubed
2 cups (7 ounces) elbow macaroni   1/2 cup water
1 28-ounce can tomatoes   1 teaspoon salt
1 12-ounce can whole kernel   1/4 teaspoon pepper
  corn

Brown meat; drain. Add onion; cook until tender. Stir in remaining
ingredients. Cover; simmer 30 minutes, stirring occasionally.
6 to 8 servings

Opposite: Broccoli and Corn Scallop (page 64), Parmesan Tomato Bake (page 64)

Chapter 4
Zesty Vegetables

Broccoli and Corn Scallop

2 tablespoons chopped onion
Parkay margarine
1 tablespoon flour
1 1/4 cups milk
1 8-ounce package shredded
  Casino brand natural
  monterey jack cheese

1 12-ounce can whole kernel
  corn, drained
1/2 cup cracker crumbs
2 10-ounce packages frozen
  broccoli spears, cooked,
  drained

Sauté onion in 1 tablespoon margarine; blend in flour. Gradually add milk; cook, stirring constantly, until thickened. Add cheese, stirring until melted. Stir in corn and 1/4 cup crumbs. Arrange broccoli in 11 3/4 x 7 1/2-inch baking dish. Pour cheese sauce over broccoli. Toss remaining crumbs with 1 tablespoon melted margarine; sprinkle over casserole. Bake at 350°, 30 minutes.   8 servings

To make ahead: Cover and refrigerate overnight. Bake, uncovered, at 350°, 45 minutes.

Parmesan Tomato Bake

1 16-ounce can stewed tomatoes
1 tablespoon cornstarch
1 8-ounce can small whole onions,
  drained

3/4 cup (3 ounces) Kraft
  grated parmesan cheese
1 egg
Dash of salt

Combine tomatoes and cornstarch. Cook over medium heat until clear and thickened. Stir in onions. Pour vegetables into 1-quart casserole. Combine cheese, egg and salt; mix well. Spoon rounded teaspoonfuls of cheese mixture around edge of casserole. Bake at 350°, 20 minutes.   4 to 6 servings

Gold Coast Potatoes

4 large baked potatoes
1 1/2 cups (6 ounces) shredded
  Kraft sharp natural cheddar
  cheese
1/4 cup milk
1/4 cup Miracle Whip salad
  dressing

1 egg
1/2 teaspoon salt
Dash of pepper
Green onion slices
Crisply cooked bacon slices,
  crumbled

Cut a lengthwise slice from top of each potato; scoop out center to form a shell. Mash potatoes; add 1 cup cheese, milk, salad dressing, egg and seasonings. Beat until fluffy; fill shells. Place on cookie sheet. Bake at 350°, 15 minutes. Top with remaining cheese, onion and bacon; continue baking 15 minutes.   4 servings

Potatoes Ranchero

1/4 cup Parkay margarine
1/4 cup flour
2 cups milk
1 teaspoon salt
Dash of pepper

2 cups (8 ounces) shredded Kraft
  sharp natural cheddar cheese
1/2 cup green onion slices
6 cups cooked potato slices
1 green pepper, cut into rings
1/4 cup Kraft barbecue sauce

Make a white sauce with margarine, flour, milk and seasonings. Add cheese and onion; stir until cheese melts. Layer half of potatoes and cheese sauce in 11 3/4 x 7 1/2-inch baking dish; repeat layers. Top with green pepper; drizzle with barbecue sauce. Bake at 350°, 25 to 30 minutes or until hot.   8 servings

Confetti Potato Bake

2 cups hot mashed potatoes
1 cup (4 ounces) shredded Kraft
  sharp natural cheddar cheese
2 tablespoons chopped pimiento

1 tablespoon chopped chives
1/2 teaspoon salt
Dash of pepper
Tomato wedges

Combine potatoes, 3/4 cup cheese, pimiento, chives and seasonings. Place in 1-quart greased casserole. Bake at 350°, 25 minutes. Top with tomato wedges and remaining cheese; continue cooking until cheese is melted.   6 servings

Easy Potatoes au Gratin

3 1/2 cups potato slices

1 8-ounce jar Cheez Whiz
  pasteurized process cheese
  spread

Place potatoes in 1-quart casserole. Heat process cheese spread over low heat; pour over potatoes. Cover; bake at 350°, 45 minutes. Uncover; continue baking 15 minutes.   6 servings

Au Gratin Potatoes Parmesan

1/4 cup Parkay margarine
2 tablespoons flour
1 cup milk
1/2 teaspoon salt
Dash of pepper

1/4 cup (1 ounce) Kraft
  grated parmesan cheese
1/2 teaspoon dill weed
3 cups cooked potato slices
1/4 cup dry bread crumbs

Make a white sauce with 2 tablespoons margarine, flour, milk and seasonings. Stir in cheese and dill. Combine sauce and potatoes; pour into 1-quart casserole. Top with crumbs tossed with 2 tablespoons melted margarine. Bake at 350°, 25 minutes.
4 to 6 servings

Golden Puffed Potatoes

Baked potatoes
Parkay margarine
Milk

Salt and pepper
Velveeta pasteurized process
   cheese spread, cubed

Slice tops from baked potatoes; scoop out insides. For each potato, add 1 tablespoon margarine, 1 tablespoon milk and seasonings. Beat until fluffy. Stir in process cheese spread. Fill shell; place on cookie sheet. Bake at 375°, 20 minutes or until lightly browned.

Creamy Potatoes and Peas

2 4-ounce containers Philadelphia
   Brand Whipped cream cheese
   with chives
1/4 cup milk

3 cups hot cooked potato slices
1 10-ounce package frozen peas,
   cooked, drained

Combine Whipped cream cheese with milk. Cook over low heat, stirring until sauce is smooth. Combine hot vegetables and sauce. 6 servings

---

An easy way to add flavor to vegetables is to stir in your favorite flavor of whipped cream cheese. Add whipped cream cheese with bacon and horseradish to hot green beans or try whipped cream cheese with chives with hot green peas. Heat thoroughly over low heat before serving.

Party Potatoes

Parkay margarine
1/4 cup flour
1/2 teaspoon salt
1/2 teaspoon dry mustard
1/4 teaspoon pepper
1 1/2 cups milk

1/2 pound Velveeta pasteurized
   process cheese spread, cubed
1 1/2 cups chopped ham
2 tablespoons chopped onion
4 cups cooked potato slices
1/2 cup cracker crumbs

Melt 1/4 cup margarine in saucepan over low heat. Blend in flour and seasonings. Gradually add milk; cook, stirring constantly, until thickened. Add process cheese spread; stir until melted. Stir in ham and onion. Alternate layers of potatoes and sauce in 2-quart casserole. Top with cracker crumbs tossed with 2 tablespoons melted margarine. Bake at 350°, 30 minutes.   6 servings

Opposite: Golden Puffed Potatoes

Cheesy Potato Puff

1 5-ounce jar Old English sharp
pasteurized process cheese
spread
2 eggs, separated

2 tablespoons chopped pimiento
1 tablespoon chopped fresh parsley
4 cups hot mashed potatoes

Add process cheese spread, egg yolks, pimiento and parsley to
potatoes; mix well. Fold in stiffly beaten egg whites. Pour into
1 1/2-quart casserole; bake at 350°, 55 minutes.   6 to 8 servings

Cheddar-Spinach Pie

2 cups (8 ounces) shredded Kraft
sharp natural cheddar cheese
2 tablespoons flour
4 eggs, beaten
1 cup milk

1/4 teaspoon salt
Dash of pepper
1 10-ounce package frozen
chopped spinach, cooked,
drained

Toss cheese with flour. Combine eggs, milk and seasonings; add
cheese mixture and spinach. Mix well. Pour into greased 9-inch pie
plate. Bake at 350°, 40 minutes.   8 servings

Spinach Treat

1 8-ounce package Philadelphia
Brand cream cheese, cubed
2 tablespoons Parkay margarine
3/4 teaspoon salt
1/4 teaspoon Tabasco sauce

2 tablespoons milk
2 10-ounce packages frozen
chopped spinach, cooked,
drained
1 hard-cooked egg, finely chopped

Heat cream cheese, margarine, salt, Tabasco sauce and milk over
low heat, stirring until smooth. Add spinach; heat. Top with egg.
6 to 8 servings

Simple Spinach Puff

1 16-ounce jar Cheez Whiz
pasteurized process cheese
spread
2 tablespoons flour

4 eggs, separated
1 10-ounce package frozen
chopped spinach, cooked,
well drained

Cook process cheese spread over low heat. Remove from heat;
blend in flour and egg yolks. Stir in spinach. Fold in stiffly beaten
egg whites. Pour into greased 10 x 6-inch baking dish. Bake at 350°,
25 to 30 minutes or until golden brown.   6 to 8 servings

> Remember, cheese sauce can turn plain vegetables into a special
> company treat.

Sunday Best Beans

6 bacon slices
1/4 cup chopped onion
2 9-ounce packages frozen cut
    green beans, cooked, drained

1 8-ounce jar Cheez Whiz
    pasteurized process cheese
    spread
1 4-ounce can mushrooms, drained

Fry bacon until crisp; remove from skillet. Drain fat, reserving 1 tablespoon. Crumble bacon. Cook onion in reserved bacon fat; add bacon, green beans, process cheese spread and mushrooms. Heat, stirring occasionally.   6 to 8 servings

Supreme Green Beans

4 cups fresh cut green beans or
    2 9-ounce packages frozen
    cut green beans
1/2 teaspoon dill weed
1 teaspoon dry mustard

1/2 pound Velveeta pasteurized
    process cheese spread, cubed
6 crisply cooked bacon slices,
    crumbled

Cook beans with dill; drain. Add mustard and process cheese spread; mix lightly. Place in 1-quart casserole; top with bacon. Bake at 350°, 15 minutes. Stir before serving.   6 to 8 servings

Pleasin' Green Beans

1/2 pound Velveeta pasteurized
    process cheese spread, cubed
1/4 cup milk

4 cups fresh whole green beans or
    2 9-ounce packages frozen
    whole green beans
1 4-ounce can mushrooms, drained

Cook process cheese spread and milk over low heat; stir until smooth. Cook green beans; add mushrooms and heat. Drain. Pour sauce over beans and mushrooms.   6 servings

Golden Green Pepper Bake

3 green peppers, cut in half
1/2 pound Velveeta pasteurized
    process cheese spread, cubed
1 12-ounce can whole kernel
    corn, drained

1 cup chopped tomato
1 cup fresh bread crumbs
2 tablespoons Parkay margarine,
    melted

Remove seeds from peppers; parboil 5 minutes. Drain. Reserve 1/2 cup process cheese spread. Combine remaining process cheese spread, corn and tomato. Spoon mixture into peppers; top with reserved process cheese spread and crumbs tossed with margarine. Place peppers in baking dish; bake at 350°, 30 to 35 minutes, or until crumbs are golden brown.   6 servings

Green Peppers Romano

3 green peppers, cut in half
1 1/2 cups zucchini slices
1 tablespoon Parkay margarine
1 12-ounce can whole kernel
   corn, drained

1 cup chopped tomato
1/4 teaspoon salt
1/8 teaspoon oregano
Kraft grated romano cheese

Remove seeds from peppers; parboil 5 minutes. Drain. Sauté
zucchini in margarine. Combine zucchini, corn, tomato and
seasonings. Spoon mixture into peppers. Place pepper halves in
baking dish; bake at 350°, 30 to 35 minutes or until hot. Sprinkle
with cheese before serving.   6 servings

Add extra flavor to broiled tomatoes by sprinkling tomato halves
with grated parmesan cheese or shredded cheddar cheese a few
minutes before the tomatoes have finished cooking. Return the
tomato halves to the broiler just long enough to melt the cheese.

Vegetables Romano

3 medium zucchini, sliced
1 cup onion rings
3 tablespoons Parkay margarine

1/2 teaspoon salt
1 cup chopped tomato
Kraft grated romano cheese

Sauté zucchini and onion in margarine 10 minutes. Add salt and
tomato; continue cooking over low heat 5 minutes. Sprinkle with
cheese before serving.   4 to 6 servings

Genoese Zucchini

3 medium zucchini
3 bacon slices
1/4 cup chopped onion
1 1/2 cups (6 ounces) shredded
   Casino brand natural low
   moisture part-skim mozzarella
   cheese

1/2 cup chopped tomato
1/4 teaspoon salt

Parboil zucchini 10 minutes. Cut in half lengthwise. Scoop out
centers; chop and drain. Fry bacon until crisp; remove from skillet,
reserving fat. Cook onion in bacon fat until tender; drain. Combine
onion, chopped zucchini, cheese, tomato and salt; mix lightly. Fill
zucchini shells. Place in 11 3/4 x 7 1/2-inch baking dish. Crumble
bacon; sprinkle over top. Bake at 350°, 30 to 35 minutes or until
hot.   6 servings

Mashed potatoes, flavored with two kinds of cheese — cheddar and
parmesan or colby and muenster — are a delightful addition to a
dinner menu.

Zucchini and Mac Bake

1 medium zucchini, sliced
1/4 cup Parkay margarine
1/4 cup flour
1/2 teaspoon salt
1/2 teaspoon oregano
1/4 teaspoon garlic salt

2 cups milk
2 cups (8 ounces) shredded Kraft
    sharp natural cheddar cheese
2 cups (7 ounces) elbow
    macaroni, cooked, drained
1/2 cup chopped tomato

Sauté zucchini in margarine; blend in flour and seasonings. Gradually add milk; cook, stirring constantly, until thickened. Add 1 1/2 cups cheese; stir until melted. Stir in macaroni and tomato; pour into 1 1/2-quart casserole. Bake at 350°, 25 minutes. Top with remaining cheese; continue baking until cheese melts.
6 servings

> Spoon sour cream dip with French onion over opened baked potatoes to make the ideal accompaniment for hamburgers or steak.

County Fair Broccoli

1/3 cup chopped onion
1 tablespoon Parkay margarine
4 eggs, beaten
1/4 cup milk
1/4 teaspoon salt
Dash of pepper

1 10-ounce package frozen
    chopped broccoli, cooked,
    drained
1/2 cup (2 ounces) Kraft
    grated parmesan cheese

Sauté onion in margarine. Combine eggs, milk and seasonings; stir in onion, broccoli and cheese. Pour into greased 9-inch pie plate; bake at 350°, 15 to 20 minutes or until set. Serve immediately.
6 to 8 servings

> Baked potatoes are delicious when opened and topped with Cheez Whiz pasteurized process cheese spread. Sprinkle with chopped chives or green onion slices for additional flavor and color.

Scalloped Green Peas and Onions

1/4 cup Parkay margarine
1/4 cup flour
2 cups milk
1/2 teaspoon salt
Dash of pepper

3 cups quartered small onions
1 10-ounce package frozen
    peas, partially thawed
1 cup (4 ounces) shredded
    Kraft natural Swiss cheese

Make a white sauce with margarine, flour, milk and seasonings. Combine onions and peas. Place in greased 10 x 6-inch baking dish. Pour sauce over vegetables; top with cheese. Bake at 375°, 45 minutes.   6 servings

Vegetable Special

1 9-ounce package frozen cut
  green beans, cooked, drained
1 10-ounce package frozen
  cauliflower, cooked, drained

1 5-ounce jar Kraft pasteurized
  process cheese spread with
  garlic
1/2 cup French fried onions

Combine hot green beans, hot cauliflower and process cheese
spread; mix well. Top with onions before serving. 6 servings

Eastern Vegetable Bouquet

1 16-ounce can bean sprouts,
  drained
1 9-ounce package frozen cut
  green beans, cooked, drained
1 6-ounce can water chestnuts,
  drained, sliced

1/2 pound Velveeta pasteurized
  process cheese spread, cubed
1/2 cup dairy sour cream
1 1/2 teaspoons soy sauce

Combine vegetables; mix lightly and heat. Heat process cheese
spread, sour cream and soy sauce over low heat. Stir until sauce is
smooth. Serve over hot vegetables. 8 servings

Golden Fried Rice

1 cup green onion slices
1/4 cup Parkay margarine
2 eggs, beaten
4 cups cooked rice
1 16-ounce can bean sprouts,
  drained

1 4-ounce can mushrooms, drained
1/4 cup slivered almonds, toasted
2 tablespoons soy sauce
1 8-ounce jar Cheez Whiz
  pasteurized process cheese
  spread

In a 12-inch skillet, sauté onion in margarine; push to side of skillet.
Add eggs and cook until just set. Stir onion into eggs. Add rice,
bean sprouts, mushrooms, almonds and soy sauce. Cook, stirring
lightly, until hot. Stir in process cheese spread; heat. Serve immediately. 8 to 10 servings

Tomato and Corn Scallop

1 8-ounce jar Cheez Whiz
  pasteurized process cheese
  spread
1 12-ounce can whole kernel
  corn, drained

3/4 cup cracker crumbs
3 medium tomatoes, sliced
1 tablespoon Parkay margarine,
  melted

Cook process cheese spread in saucepan over low heat; stir in corn
and 1/2 cup crumbs. Layer half the corn mixture and tomato slices
in 8-inch baking dish; repeat layers. Toss remaining crumbs with
margarine; sprinkle over casserole. Bake at 350°, 30 minutes.
4 to 6 servings

Opposite: Wilted Spinach Salad (page 74), Potato Salad Debonair (page 74)

Chapter 5
Special Salads and
Salad Dressings

Wilted Spinach Salad

1/3 cup Kraft herb and garlic
  or Italian dressing
2 tablespoons finely chopped
  onion
1/4 teaspoon pepper
6 cups spinach

4 crisply cooked bacon slices,
  crumbled
1/2 cup (2 ounces) Kraft grated
  parmesan cheese
1 hard-cooked egg, chopped

Combine dressing, onion and pepper; heat. Tear spinach in bite-size pieces into salad bowl. Add crumbled bacon and cheese. Toss with dressing. Top with egg.   6 servings

Potato Salad Debonair

4 cups chopped cooked potatoes
1/2 cup Miracle Whip salad
  dressing
1/2 cup dairy sour cream
2 cups (8 ounces) cubed Kraft
  sharp natural cheddar cheese

1 cup celery slices
1 cup cooked carrot slices
3 hard-cooked eggs, sliced
1/4 cup green onion slices
2 teaspoons salt
1 teaspoon prepared mustard

Combine all ingredients; mix lightly. Chill.   6 to 8 servings

Swiss Chicken Salad

2 cups chopped cooked chicken
1 8-ounce can crushed pineapple,
  drained
1 6-ounce package Kraft shredded
  natural Swiss cheese

3/4 cup celery slices
1/2 teaspoon salt
Dash of pepper
Kraft real mayonnaise

Combine chicken, pineapple, cheese, celery, seasonings and enough mayonnaise to moisten; mix lightly. Chill.   4 servings

---

For a special treat, place a spoonful of whipped cream cheese on top of a gelatin fruit salad.

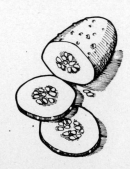

Chicken 'n Parm Salad

3 cups chopped cooked chicken
1 cup chopped cucumber
1/2 cup (2 ounces) Kraft grated
  parmesan cheese

1/4 cup green onion slices
2 tablespoons chopped pimiento
1/2 teaspoon salt
3/4 cup Kraft real mayonnaise

Combine all ingredients except mayonnaise; toss lightly. Add mayonnaise; mix well. Chill. Add additional mayonnaise before serving, if desired.   4 servings

Bayside Salad

1 16-ounce can whole green
  beans, drained
1/4 pound Velveeta pasteurized
  process cheese spread, cubed

1 cup onion rings
1/2 cup Catalina brand French
  dressing
2 tablespoons chopped pimiento

Combine all ingredients; toss lightly. Chill.   4 servings

Tanglewood Bean Salad

1 16-ounce can cut green beans,
  drained
1 16-ounce can lima beans, drained
1 16-ounce can kidney beans,
  drained
2 cups (8 ounces) cubed Kraft
  sharp natural cheddar cheese

1 cup chopped tomato
6 crisply cooked bacon slices,
  crumbled
Golden Caesar dressing from
  Kraft

Combine beans, cheese, tomato, bacon and enough dressing to moisten; mix lightly. Chill.   10 to 12 servings

Chef's salad is a popular favorite. To make it, cut thin strips of cheese (cheddar, Swiss or brick) and thin strips of cooked chicken or ham. Place the strips of cheese and meat on top of mixed greens and add the dressing.

Four Seasons Bean Salad

1 16-ounce can kidney beans,
  drained
1 16-ounce can cut green beans,
  drained
2 cups (8 ounces) cubed Kraft
  sharp natural cheddar cheese
6 hard-cooked eggs, sliced

1 cup celery slices
1/2 cup onion rings
3/4 cup Kraft thousand island
  dressing
1 teaspoon salt
Dash of pepper

Combine all ingredients; mix lightly. Chill.   8 servings

Pink Sparkle Freeze

1/4 cup honey
1 8-ounce package Philadelphia
  Brand cream cheese
1 8 1/4-ounce can crushed
  pineapple, undrained

1 10-ounce package frozen
  strawberries, thawed
1 cup heavy cream, whipped

Gradually add honey to softened cream cheese, mixing until well
blended. Stir in fruit; fold in whipped cream. Pour into six 3/4-cup
molds; freeze until firm. Unmold.   6 servings

Creamy Blue Cheese Salad

1 envelope unflavored gelatin
1 cup cold water
1 8-ounce package Philadelphia
  Brand cream cheese
1 cup (4 ounces) crumbled
  Casino brand natural blue
  cheese

1 cup cottage cheese
1/4 teaspoon onion salt
1/8 teaspoon celery salt
1/8 teaspoon paprika

Soften gelatin in 1/2 cup water. Stir over low heat until dissolved;
add remaining water. Combine softened cream cheese and remaining ingredients; mix well. Gradually add gelatin mixture to cream
cheese mixture, mixing until well blended. Pour into lightly oiled
1-quart mold; chill until firm. Unmold.   8 to 10 servings

Golden Potato Salad

1/2 cup Cheez Whiz pasteurized
  process cheese spread
1/4 cup dairy sour cream
4 cups chopped cooked potatoes
4 hard-cooked eggs, chopped

1 cup celery slices
1/4 cup chopped green pepper
1/4 cup chopped onion
1/2 teaspoon salt

Combine process cheese spread and sour cream; mix well. Combine potatoes, eggs, celery, green pepper, onion and salt. Add
process cheese spread mixture; mix lightly. Chill.   6 to 8 servings

Ham and Cheese Potato Salad

4 cups chopped cooked potatoes
4 hard-cooked eggs, chopped
1 cup celery slices
1 cup cubed cooked ham
3/4 cup (3 ounces) Kraft
  grated parmesan cheese

1/4 cup chopped onion
1/4 cup chopped green pepper
1 teaspoon salt
Miracle Whip salad dressing

Combine potatoes, eggs, celery, ham, cheese, onion, green pepper, salt and enough salad dressing to moisten; mix lightly. Chill. Sprinkle with additional cheese, if desired.   6 to 8 servings

Hot Parmesan Potato Salad

4 cups cooked potato slices
1/2 cup celery slices
1/4 cup green onion slices
8 crisply cooked bacon slices,
  crumbled

1/3 cup Kraft Italian dressing
1/2 cup (2 ounces) Kraft grated
  parmesan cheese

Combine potatoes, celery, onion and bacon. Toss with dressing. Cook over low heat, stirring occasionally. Remove from heat; stir in cheese. Serve hot. Top with additional cheese, if desired.
4 to 6 servings

Add cubes of Velveeta pasteurized process cheese spread to green bean salad for extra flavor.

Cranberry Buffet Mold

2 envelopes unflavored gelatin
1 cup cranberry juice
1 10-ounce package frozen
  cranberry-orange relish,
  thawed
1 cup cold water
1 cup Miracle Whip salad
  dressing

1 8-ounce package Philadelphia
  Brand cream cheese
2 cups chopped cooked chicken
  or turkey
1/2 cup celery slices

Soften 1 envelope of gelatin in cranberry juice; stir over low heat until dissolved. Cool. Stir in relish. Pour into lightly oiled 2-quart mold; chill until almost set.

Soften remaining envelope of gelatin in water; stir over low heat until dissolved. Cool. Gradually add salad dressing and gelatin to softened cream cheese, mixing until well blended. Stir in chicken and celery. Pour over cranberry layer; chill until firm. Unmold.
6 to 8 servings

Lemon-Lime Tropical Mold

1   8 1/4-ounce can crushed
    pineapple
1 3-ounce package lime flavored
    gelatin
1 cup boiling water
1 cup cold water
1/4 cup chopped pecans

*   *   *

1 3-ounce package lemon flavored
    gelatin
1 1/2 cups boiling water
1 8-ounce package Philadelphia
    Brand cream cheese

Drain pineapple, reserving 1/4 cup syrup. Dissolve lime gelatin in boiling water; add cold water. Chill until partially set; fold in pineapple and nuts. Pour into lightly oiled 1 1/2-quart mold; chill until almost set.

Dissolve lemon gelatin in water; add reserved syrup. Gradually add to softened cream cheese, mixing until well blended. Pour over lime layer; chill until firm. Unmold.   6 to 8 servings

Frothy Lime Pear Mold

1 3-ounce package lime
    flavored gelatin
1 cup boiling water
1/2 cup cold water
1/2 cup Kraft pure 100%
    pasteurized orange juice
1 17-ounce can pear halves

*   *   *

1 3-ounce package lemon
    flavored gelatin
1 cup boiling water
3/4 cup cold water
2 tablespoons lemon juice
1 8-ounce package Philadelphia
    Brand cream cheese

Dissolve lime gelatin in boiling water; add cold water and orange juice. Arrange pear halves in lightly oiled 6-cup ring mold; cover with gelatin. Chill until almost set.

Dissolve lemon gelatin in boiling water; add cold water and lemon juice. Gradually add to softened cream cheese, mixing until well blended. Pour over lime layer. Chill until firm. Unmold.
6 to 8 servings

Opposite: Lemon-Lime Tropical Mold

Empress Mold

1 3-ounce package lime
  flavored gelatin
1 cup boiling water
3/4 cup cold water

1 8-ounce package Philadelphia
  Brand cream cheese
1 16-ounce can peach slices,
  drained

Dissolve gelatin in boiling water; add cold water. Gradually add to softened cream cheese, mixing until well blended. Chill until partially set. Fold in peaches; pour into 1-quart mold. Chill until firm. Unmold.   6 servings

Hot Chicken Salad with Cheese

3 cups chopped cooked chicken
1 1/2 cups celery slices
1/4 cup chopped pitted ripe
  olives
2 tablespoons finely chopped
  onion

1/2 cup Miracle Whip salad
  dressing
2 tablespoons milk
1 teaspoon salt
1 cup (4 ounces) shredded Kraft
  sharp natural cheddar cheese

Combine all ingredients except cheese; mix lightly. Place in 1-quart casserole. Bake at 350°, 50 minutes. Top with cheese; continue baking until cheese melts.   4 servings

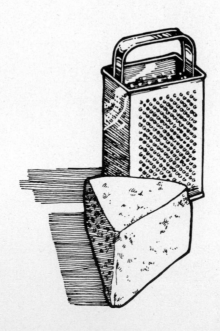

Macaroni and Cheese Salad

2 cups (7 ounces) elbow
  macaroni, cooked, drained
1 10-ounce package frozen peas,
  cooked, drained
1/2 pound Kraft American
  pasteurized process cheese,
  cubed

1/2 cup chopped celery
1/2 cup Miracle Whip salad
  dressing
2 tablespoons chopped onion
1/2 teaspoon salt
Dash of pepper

Combine all ingredients; mix lightly. Chill. Add additional salad dressing just before serving, if desired. 8 to 10 servings

Hearty Mac Salad

2 cups (7 ounces) elbow
  macaroni, cooked, drained
1 8-ounce package Kraft sharp
  natural cheddar cheese, cubed
3/4 cup Miracle Whip salad
  dressing
1/2 cup celery slices

1/2 cup chopped cooked ham
2 tablespoons chopped pimiento
1 tablespoon chopped green
  pepper
1 tablespoon chopped onion
1/4 teaspoon salt
Dash of pepper

Combine macaroni, cheese, 1/2 cup salad dressing, celery, ham, pimiento, green pepper, onion and seasonings; toss lightly. Chill. Add remaining salad dressing before serving. 6 servings

Variation: Replace ham with 3 crisply cooked bacon slices, crumbled.

Mac and Parm Salad

2 cups (7 ounces) elbow
  macaroni, cooked, drained
1 cup chopped tomato
3/4 cup celery slices
1/2 cup (2 ounces) Kraft grated
  parmesan cheese

1/3 cup chopped onion
1/3 cup chopped dill pickle
1 teaspoon prepared mustard
Dash of pepper
3/4 cup Kraft real mayonnaise

Combine all ingredients except mayonnaise; toss lightly. Add mayonnaise; mix well. Chill. Add additional mayonnaise and sprinkle with additional cheese before serving, if desired.
6 to 8 servings

Macaroni Picnic Salad

2 cups (7 ounces) elbow
   macaroni, cooked, drained
1 cup chopped tomato
1/2 cup chopped green pepper
1/4 cup chopped onion

1/2 teaspoon garlic salt
1 8-ounce jar Cheez Whiz
   pasteurized process cheese
   spread

Combine hot macaroni, tomato, green pepper, onion and garlic salt; toss lightly. Add process cheese spread; stir until well blended. Chill.   6 servings

---

Shreds of whatever cheese you have on hand (cheddar, Swiss or brick) make a flavorful addition to a crisp tossed salad.

Patio Tuna Salad

2 6 1/2-ounce cans tuna, drained,
   flaked
1 cup celery slices
1 cup grape halves
1 8-ounce can pineapple chunks,
   drained

1/2 pound Velveeta pasteurized
   process cheese spread, cubed
Miracle Whip salad dressing

Combine tuna, celery, grapes, pineapple, process cheese spread and enough salad dressing to moisten; mix lightly.   4 to 6 servings

Mohave Fruit Salad

2 cups chopped apples
1 1/2 cups (6 ounces) cubed Kraft
  sharp natural cheddar cheese
1 cup orange sections
1/2 cup chopped dates

1/2 cup chopped walnuts
1/2 cup Miracle Whip salad
  dressing
1 teaspoon grated orange rind
1 teaspoon lemon juice

Combine all ingredients; mix lightly. Chill.   4 to 6 servings

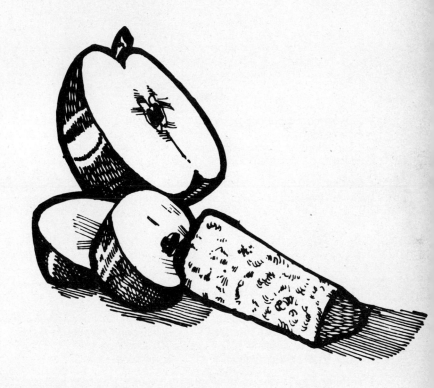

Waldorf Swiss Salad

3 cups chopped apples
1 cup chopped celery
1/2 cup chopped walnuts
1/2 cup raisins

1 6-ounce package Kraft shredded
  natural Swiss cheese
Miracle Whip salad dressing

Combine apples, celery, nuts, raisins, cheese and enough salad
dressing to moisten; mix lightly. Serve immediately.   6 servings

Salad Olé

3 cups iceberg lettuce chunks
1 tomato, chopped
1 avocado, peeled, cubed
1 cup (4 ounces) cubed Kraft
sharp natural cheddar cheese

1/4 cup chopped onion
Catalina brand French dressing
1 cup corn chips

Combine lettuce, tomato, avocado, cheese, onion and enough dressing to moisten; toss lightly. Serve topped with corn chips.
6 servings

Snappy Slaw

3 cups shredded cabbage
1/4 cup radish slices
1/4 cup chopped green pepper
2 tablespoons chopped onion

1 cup (4 ounces) cubed Kraft
sharp natural cheddar cheese
Kraft coleslaw dressing

Combine cabbage, radishes, green pepper, onion, cheese and enough dressing to moisten; mix lightly. Chill.   6 servings

Continental Egg Salad

6 hard-cooked eggs, chopped
1 1/2 cups (6 ounces) shredded
Kraft natural Swiss cheese
1/2 cup Kraft real mayonnaise

1 tablespoon freeze-dried chives
1 teaspoon prepared mustard
1/2 teaspoon salt
6 tomatoes

Combine eggs, cheese, mayonnaise, chives, mustard and salt. Cut each tomato in six sections almost to stem end. Fill with egg mixture.   6 servings

Creamy Fruit Dressing

1/4 cup honey
1/4 cup Kraft pure 100%
   pasteurized orange juice
2 tablespoons lemon juice

Dash of salt
1 8-ounce package Philadelphia
   Brand cream cheese
1/2 cup all purpose oil

Combine honey, juices and salt. Gradually add to softened cream cheese, mixing until well blended. Add oil, 2 tablespoons at a time, beating well after each addition. Chill.   2 cups

Ginger-Orange Fruit Dressing

1 8-ounce package Philadelphia
   Brand cream cheese
1/4 cup Kraft pure 100%
   pasteurized orange juice

1 tablespoon sugar
1/2 teaspoon ginger

Combine softened cream cheese and remaining ingredients. Mix until well blended.   2 cups

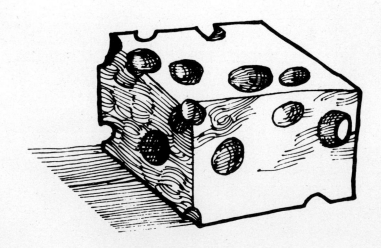

Roquefort Dressing Supreme

1 8-ounce package Philadelphia
  Brand cream cheese
3/4 cup (3 ounces) Louis Rigal
  roquefort cheese
3/4 cup milk

1/4 cup Kraft real mayonnaise
3 tablespoons lemon juice
2 tablespoons chopped chives
1 teaspoon Worcestershire sauce
Dash of Tabasco sauce

Combine softened cream cheese and roquefort cheese, mixing until well blended. Gradually stir in remaining ingredients; mix well. Chill.   2 1/2 cups

Creamy Blue Cheese Dressing

1 6-ounce package crumbled
  Casino brand natural blue
  cheese
1 cup Kraft real mayonnaise

3/4 cup buttermilk
1/4 teaspoon onion powder
Dash of garlic powder

Combine ingredients, mixing until well blended.   2 cups

Opposite: Bavarian Apple Torte (page 88), Marble Cheese Cake (page 88)

Chapter 6
Savory Sweets

Bavarian Apple Torte

1/2 cup Parkay margarine
1/3 cup sugar
1/4 teaspoon vanilla
1 cup flour

*   *   *

1 8-ounce package Philadelphia
   Brand cream cheese
1/4 cup sugar

1 egg
1/2 teaspoon vanilla

*   *   *

1/3 cup sugar
1/2 teaspoon cinnamon
4 cups peeled thin apple slices
1/4 cup sliced almonds

Cream margarine, sugar and vanilla. Blend in flour. Spread dough onto bottom and 2 inches high around sides of 9-inch springform pan.

Combine softened cream cheese and sugar; mix well. Add egg and vanilla; mix well. Pour into pastry-lined pan.

Combine sugar and cinnamon. Toss apples in sugar mixture. Spoon apple mixture over cream cheese layer; sprinkle with nuts. Bake at 450°, 10 minutes. Reduce oven temperature to 400°; continue baking 25 minutes. Cool before removing rim of pan.
8 to 10 servings

Marble Cheesecake

1 cup graham cracker crumbs
3 tablespoons sugar
3 tablespoons Parkay margarine,
   melted

*   *   *

3 8-ounce packages Philadelphia
   Brand cream cheese

3/4 cup sugar
3 tablespoons flour
1 teaspoon vanilla
3 eggs
1 1-ounce square unsweetened
   chocolate, melted

Combine crumbs, sugar and margarine. Press onto bottom of 9-inch springform pan. Bake at 350°, 10 minutes. Increase oven temperature to 450°.

Combine softened cream cheese, sugar, flour and vanilla, mixing at medium speed on electric mixer until well blended. Add eggs, one at a time, mixing well after each addition. Add melted chocolate to 1 cup of batter; mix until well blended. Spoon plain and chocolate batters alternately over crust; cut through batter with knife several times for marble effect. Bake at 450°, 10 minutes. Reduce oven temperature to 250°, continue baking 30 minutes. Loosen cake from rim of pan; cool before removing rim. Chill.
10 servings

Vanilla "Philly" Frosting

1 8-ounce package Philadelphia
  Brand cream cheese
1 tablespoon milk
1 teaspoon vanilla

Dash of salt
5 1/2 cups sifted confectioners'
  sugar

Combine softened cream cheese, milk, vanilla and salt, mixing until well blended. Add sugar, 1 cup at a time, mixing well after each addition.   Fills and frosts two 8 or 9-inch cake layers

Variations: Substitute 1 teaspoon almond extract for vanilla.
               Stir in 1/4 cup crushed peppermint candy.
               Stir in 1/4 cup crushed lemon drops and 1 teaspoon lemon juice.

Fruit and cheese are a popular continental dessert. Accompany crisp slices of apple with wedges of sharp cheddar cheese — green grapes with chunks of Swiss cheese, or pears with brick or muenster cheese slices.

"Philly" Fruit Cake

1 8-ounce package Philadelphia
  Brand cream cheese
1/2 cup Parkay margarine
1 cup sugar
3 eggs
2 1/2 cups flour
1 teaspoon baking powder
1 teaspoon salt

1/2 cup Kraft pure 100%
  pasteurized orange juice
1 1/2 cups mixed diced
  candied fruit
1 1/4 cups (8 ounces) pitted
  dates, chopped
1 cup chopped pecans

Combine softened cream cheese, margarine and sugar; mix well. Add eggs, one at a time, mixing well after each addition. Combine 2 cups flour, baking powder and salt; add to creamed mixture, alternately with orange juice, mixing well after each addition. Toss fruit and nuts in remaining flour; fold into batter. Pour into greased and floured 10-inch tube pan. Bake at 300°, 1 hour and 45 minutes. Cool 5 minutes; remove from pan. Cool completely.

Variation: To moisten with brandy, wrap cake in cheese cloth moistened with 1/2 cup brandy. Wrap tightly in heavy duty foil and store in a cool, dry place for 1 week. Repeat, moistening cloth with 1/4 cup brandy and store 1 week. Repeat, moistening cloth with 1/4 cup brandy. Store an additional 5 to 7 days before serving.

Chocolate "Philly" Fudge

4 cups sifted confectioners'
  sugar
1 8-ounce package Philadelphia
  Brand cream cheese
4 1-ounce squares unsweetened
  chocolate, melted

1 teaspoon vanilla
Dash of salt
1/2 cup chopped nuts

Gradually add sugar to softened cream cheese, mixing until well blended. Stir in remaining ingredients. Spread into greased 8-inch square pan. Chill several hours or overnight. Cut into squares; garnish with additional nuts, if desired.   1 3/4 pounds

Variations: Peppermint "Philly" Fudge — Omit nuts and vanilla; add a few drops peppermint extract and 1/4 cup crushed peppermint candy. Sprinkle with 1/4 cup crushed peppermint candy before chilling.
       Coconut "Philly" Fudge — Omit nuts; add 1 cup shredded coconut. Garnish with additional coconut, if desired.
       Cherry "Philly" Fudge — Omit nuts; add 1/2 cup chopped maraschino cherries. Garnish with whole cherries, if desired.

Place dollops of whipped cream cheese on warm waffle squares. Then spoon hot cherry pie filling on top.

Pecan Tassies

1 3-ounce package Philadelphia
  Brand cream cheese
1/2 cup Parkay margarine
1 cup flour
     *   *   *

1 egg
3/4 cup packed brown sugar
1 teaspoon vanilla
3/4 cup chopped pecans
Confectioners' sugar

Blend softened cream cheese and margarine; stir in flour. Chill. Divide dough into 24 balls; press onto bottom and sides of miniature muffin pans.
    Combine egg, brown sugar and vanilla; stir in nuts. Fill cups 3/4 full of brown sugar mixture. Bake at 325°, 25 to 30 minutes or until light brown. Cool 5 minutes; remove from pans. Sprinkle with confectioners' sugar.   2 dozen

---

Add extra flavor to warm apple crisp by topping it with lots of shredded cheddar cheese.

Marble Squares

1/2 cup Parkay margarine
3/4 cup water
1 1/2 1-ounce squares
  unsweetened chocolate
2 cups flour
2 cups sugar
1 teaspoon soda
1/2 teaspoon salt
2 eggs

1/2 cup dairy sour cream
*   *   *
1 8-ounce package Philadelphia
  Brand cream cheese
1/3 cup sugar
1 egg
1 6-ounce package semi-sweet
  chocolate pieces

Heat margarine, water and chocolate in saucepan; bring to boil. Remove from heat. Stir in combined flour, sugar, soda and salt. Add eggs and sour cream; mix well. Pour into greased and floured 15 1/2 x 10 1/2-inch jelly roll pan.

Combine softened cream cheese and sugar, mixing until well blended. Add egg; mix well. Spoon over chocolate batter. Cut through batter with knife several times for marble effect. Sprinkle with chocolate pieces. Bake at 375°, 25 to 30 minutes or until wooden pick inserted in center comes out clean.

Fanciful Fruit Squares

1 18-ounce package refrigerated
  sugar slice and bake cookies
1 8-ounce container Philadelphia
  Brand Whipped cream cheese

1 tablespoon sugar
Assorted fruit
1/2 cup Kraft orange marmalade
2 tablespoons water

Cut cookie dough into 1/8-inch thick slices. Cover a cookie sheet with aluminum foil; arrange cookie slices, slightly overlapping, into 14 x 10-inch rectangle. Press cookie slices together lightly to seal. Bake at 375°, 10 to 12 minutes or until golden brown. Cool; remove from foil. Spread Whipped cream cheese over cookie crust; sprinkle evenly with sugar. Arrange slices of fruit over Whipped cream cheese. Glaze with combined marmalade and water. Chill; cut into squares.   10 to 12 servings

Savannah Spiced Peaches

1 29-ounce can peach halves
1/2 cup sugar
1/4 cup vinegar
1 cinnamon stick

1 teaspoon whole cloves
1/4 teaspoon ground allspice
Philadelphia Brand Whipped
  cream cheese

Drain peaches, reserving 3/4 cup syrup. Heat together syrup, vinegar and spices; simmer 10 minutes. Add peaches; cook an additional 5 minutes. Remove peaches; strain liquid to remove spices. Return peaches to liquid; serve warm, topped with Whipped cream cheese.   4 to 6 servings

Colby Apple Cobbler

1 cup sugar	1 1/2 teaspoons baking powder
1/4 cup flour	1/2 teaspoon salt
1/4 teaspoon cinnamon	1 1/2 cups (6 ounces) shredded
6 cups peeled thin apple slices	Kraft midget longhorn style
* * *	natural colby cheese
1 cup flour	1/3 cup Parkay margarine, melted
1/4 cup sugar	1/4 cup milk

Combine sugar, flour and cinnamon; toss with apples. Pour into 9-inch square pan.

Combine dry ingredients and cheese. Add margarine and milk; mix until well blended. Spoon dough over fruit mixture. Bake at 400°, 30 minutes.   6 to 8 servings

---

Top fresh strawberry, blueberry or peach shortcake with whipped cream cheese.

Chalet Swiss Cobbler

2 16-ounce cans pear halves	1 1/2 teaspoons baking powder
2 tablespoons cornstarch	1/2 teaspoon salt
1 tablespoon sugar	1 6-ounce package Kraft shredded
1/4 teaspoon cinnamon	natural Swiss cheese
1 tablespoon lemon juice	1/3 cup Parkay margarine,
* * *	melted
1 cup flour	1/4 cup milk
1/3 cup sugar	

Drain pears, reserving syrup; add enough cold water to syrup to measure 1 1/2 cups. Combine cornstarch, sugar and cinnamon in saucepan. Gradually stir in lemon juice and syrup mixture. Heat until syrup mixture thickens; boil 1 minute, stirring constantly. Place pears in 9-inch square pan; pour syrup mixture over pears.

Combine dry ingredients and cheese. Add margarine and milk; mix until well blended. Spoon dough over pears. Bake at 425°, 30 minutes.   6 to 8 servings

Variation: Substitute 1 1/2 cups (6 ounces) shredded Kraft sharp natural cheddar cheese for Swiss cheese.

Top gingerbread, warm from the oven, with whipped cream cheese. It's a quick, easy and delicious dessert.

Dulce de Taxco

1/3 cup Parkay margarine
2/3 cup packed brown sugar
1 egg
1/2 teaspoon vanilla
1 1/4 cups flour
1 1/2 teaspoons baking powder
1/2 teaspoon salt
1/2 cup milk

*　　*　　*

1 12-ounce jar Kraft caramel
  topping
1 teaspoon grated orange rind
2 bananas, sliced
Philadelphia Brand Whipped cream
  cheese
1/3 cup pecan halves

Cream margarine and sugar until light and fluffy. Blend in egg and vanilla. Add combined dry ingredients alternately with milk, mixing well after each addition. Pour into greased and floured 9-inch square pan. Bake at 350°, 25 to 30 minutes or until wooden pick inserted in center comes out clean. Cool 10 minutes; remove from pan. Cool completely.

Combine topping and rind. Cut cake into squares. Top each square with banana slices and Whipped cream cheese. Spoon topping mixture over Whipped cream cheese; sprinkle with nuts.
8 to 10 servings

Sundaes with cheese! Top slices of pound cake with slices of banana and whipped cream cheese. Then pour on the fudge sauce.

Cranberry Supreme

1 cup graham cracker crumbs
1/4 cup Parkay margarine, melted
        *　　*　　*
2 cups cranberries
1 cup granulated sugar
1/2 cup water
1/4 cup chopped nuts
2 tablespoons Kraft orange
  marmalade

*　　*　　*

1 8-ounce package Philadelphia
  Brand cream cheese
1/3 cup sifted confectioners'
  sugar
1 tablespoon milk
1 teaspoon vanilla
1 cup heavy cream, whipped

Combine crumbs and margarine; press onto bottom of 8-inch square pan.

Combine cranberries, sugar and water. Bring to a boil; simmer 20 minutes. Stir in nuts and marmalade; chill.

Combine softened cream cheese, confectioners' sugar, milk and vanilla, mixing until well blended. Fold in whipped cream; spoon over crust. Top with cranberry mixture. Chill several hours or overnight.   8 servings

Deep Dish Cranberry-Apple Pie

1 1/2 cups flour
1 1/2 teaspoons baking powder
1/4 teaspoon salt
1/4 cup Parkay margarine
1 egg, slightly beaten
1/3 cup milk
1 1/2 cups (6 ounces) shredded
Kraft sharp natural cheddar
cheese

*   *   *

1 1/2 cups sugar
1/3 cup flour
1/2 teaspoon cinnamon
6 cups peeled thin apple slices
2 cups cranberries
1 tablespoon Parkay margarine

Combine flour, baking powder and salt; cut in margarine until mixture resembles coarse crumbs. Add combined egg and milk to flour mixture. Stir in cheese; form into a ball. Roll two-thirds of dough into 15-inch square on a lightly floured surface. Line 8-inch square baking dish with dough; flute edges.

Combine sugar, flour and cinnamon. Stir in apples and cranberries. Spoon into pastry shell; dot with margarine. Roll out remaining dough to 12-inch square. Cut into 1/2-inch strips. Place strips on fruit to form lattice; press to seal. Bake at 400°, 30 minutes.   6 to 8 servings

Apricot Cream Cheese Cookies

1 cup Parkay margarine
1 3-ounce package Philadelphia
Brand cream cheese
1 cup sugar
1 egg, beaten

1 tablespoon lemon juice
1 teaspoon grated lemon rind
2 3/4 cups flour
1 teaspoon baking powder
Kraft apricot preserves

Combine margarine, softened cream cheese and sugar, mixing until well blended. Stir in egg, lemon juice and rind. Add combined dry ingredients; mix well. Chill dough. Shape level tablespoonfuls of dough into balls. Place on greased cookie sheet; flatten slightly. Indent center of each; fill with preserves. Bake at 375°, 12 to 15 minutes or until lightly browned.   4 dozen

Variation: Substitute Kraft strawberry or peach preserves for apricot preserves.

Opposite: Deep Dish Cranberry-Apple Pie

Cheddar Fruit Drops

1/2 cup Parkay margarine
1/4 cup granulated sugar
1/4 cup packed brown sugar
1 egg
1 teaspoon vanilla
1 1/2 cups flour
1/2 teaspoon soda
1/2 teaspoon salt

1 1/2 cups (6 ounces) shredded
  Cracker Barrel brand sharp
  natural cheddar cheese
1 8 1/4-ounce can crushed
  pineapple, drained
1/4 cup chopped maraschino
  cherries

Cream margarine and sugars until light and fluffy; stir in egg and
vanilla. Add combined dry ingredients; mix well. Stir in cheese,
pineapple and cherries. Drop rounded teaspoonfuls of dough onto
ungreased cookie sheet. Bake at 375°, 15 minutes.   5 dozen

Variation: Substitute 1 1/2 cups (6 ounces) of shredded Kraft
natural Swiss cheese for cheddar cheese.

Cream Cheese Spritz

1 cup Parkay margarine
1 8-ounce package Philadelphia
  Brand cream cheese
2/3 cup sugar

1 teaspoon vanilla
1 3/4 cups flour
Dash of salt

Combine margarine, softened cream cheese, sugar and vanilla,
mixing until well blended. Add flour and salt; mix well. Chill. Force
dough through cookie press onto ungreased cookie sheet. Bake at
400°, 8 to 10 minutes or until set and very slightly browned.
6 dozen

Chocolate Chipper Bars

1 8-ounce package Philadelphia
  Brand cream cheese
1/2 cup Parkay margarine
1/2 cup packed brown sugar
1/4 cup granulated sugar
1 egg
1 teaspoon vanilla
1 cup old fashioned or quick
  oats, uncooked

2/3 cup flour
1/2 teaspoon baking powder
1/4 teaspoon salt
1 6-ounce package semi-sweet
  chocolate pieces
1/4 cup chopped nuts

Combine softened cream cheese, margarine and sugars, mixing until well blended. Blend in egg and vanilla. Add combined dry ingredients; mix well. Stir in chocolate pieces and nuts. Pour into a
greased 13 x 9-inch baking pan. Bake at 350°, 30 minutes. Cool and
cut into bars.

Choco-Cherry Bars

1 8-ounce package Philadelphia
  Brand cream cheese
3/4 cup Parkay margarine
1 1/2 cups granulated sugar
2 eggs
1 teaspoon vanilla
1 1/2 cups flour
1 teaspoon baking powder
1/2 teaspoon salt
2 1-ounce squares unsweetened
  chocolate, melted

1 cup chopped maraschino
  cherries, drained
1/2 cup chopped walnuts
     *   *   *
1 cup sifted confectioners'
  sugar
2 to 3 tablespoons milk
1 1-ounce square unsweetened
  chocolate, melted
1/2 teaspoon vanilla

Combine softened cream cheese, margarine and sugar, mixing until well blended. Blend in eggs and vanilla. Add combined dry ingredients; mix well. Blend in chocolate. Stir in cherries and nuts. Spread into greased and floured 15 1/2 x 10 1/2-inch jelly roll pan. Bake at 350°, 30 minutes or until wooden pick inserted in center comes out clean.

Combine confectioners' sugar, milk, chocolate and vanilla. Drizzle over warm cookies; cool. Cut into bars.

Banana Bars

1 8-ounce package Philadelphia
  Brand cream cheese
1/2 cup Parkay margarine
1 1/2 cups packed brown sugar
1 cup mashed banana
1 egg
1/4 cup milk

2 cups flour
2 1/2 teaspoons baking powder
1 teaspoon salt
1 teaspoon cinnamon
1 cup chopped nuts
1/2 cup raisins
Confectioners' sugar

Combine softened cream cheese, margarine and brown sugar, mixing until well blended. Blend in banana, egg and milk; beat well. Add combined dry ingredients; mix well. Stir in nuts and raisins. Pour into greased and floured 15 1/2 x 10 1/2-inch jelly roll pan. Bake at 350°, 30 to 35 minutes or until wooden pick inserted in center comes out clean. Cool. Sprinkle with confectioners' sugar and cut into bars.

To make a quick, tasty dessert, spread cream cheese on slices of date-nut bread and top with slices of fresh or canned fruit.

Ambrosia Pie

1 8-ounce package Philadelphia
  Brand cream cheese
1/2 cup sugar
1 tablespoon lemon juice
2 teaspoons grated lemon rind

1 cup heavy cream, whipped
1/2 cup shredded coconut
1 1/2 cups orange sections
1 1/2 cups banana slices
1/2 cup Kraft orange marmalade

Combine softened cream cheese, sugar, lemon juice and rind, mixing until well blended. Fold in whipped cream and coconut. Spread mixture in 9-inch pie plate; spooning high around rim. Freeze. Before serving, drain orange sections. Toss fruit with marmalade; let stand 5 minutes. Fill center of cream cheese shell with fruit. Serve immediately.   6 to 8 servings

Cream Cheese Pastry

2 cups flour
1/2 teaspoon salt
1 8-ounce package Philadelphia
  Brand cream cheese

1 cup Parkay margarine

Combine flour and salt; cut in cream cheese and margarine until mixture resembles coarse crumbs. Form into ball; chill. Divide dough into 2 balls; roll each to 11-inch circle on lightly floured surface. Place in 9-inch pie plates. Flute; prick with fork. Bake at 450°, 12 to 15 minutes or until golden brown.   2 9-inch pastry shells

Variation: To make tart shells, divide dough into 16 balls. Roll each ball to 6-inch circle. Place in 4-inch tart pans. Flute; prick with fork. Bake at 450°, 8 to 10 minutes or until golden brown.   16 tart shells

Apple Cheddar Cookies

1/2 cup Parkay margarine
1/2 cup sugar
1 egg
1 teaspoon vanilla
1 1/2 cups flour
1/2 teaspoon soda
1/2 teaspoon cinnamon

1/2 teaspoon salt
1 1/2 cups (6 ounces) shredded
  Kraft sharp natural cheddar
  cheese
1 1/2 cups peeled chopped apples
1/4 cup chopped nuts

Cream margarine and sugar until light and fluffy; stir in egg and vanilla. Add combined dry ingredients; mix well. Stir in cheese, apples and nuts. Drop rounded teaspoonfuls of dough onto ungreased cookie sheet. Bake at 375°, 15 minutes.   4 1/2 dozen

Opposite: Ambrosia Pie

Elegant Cheese Cake

1 cup graham cracker crumbs
3 tablespoons sugar
3 tablespoons Parkay margarine,
   melted
            *   *   *
2 8-ounce packages Philadelphia
   Brand cream cheese

3/4 cup sugar
1/4 cup flour
2 eggs
1 cup milk
1 1/2 teaspoons vanilla

Combine crumbs, sugar and margarine; press onto bottom of 9-inch springform pan. Bake at 325°, 10 minutes.

Combine softened cream cheese, sugar and flour, mixing at medium speed on electric mixer until well blended. Add eggs, one at a time, mixing well after each addition. Blend in milk and vanilla. Pour mixture over crust. Bake at 325°, 40 minutes. Loosen cake from rim of pan; cool before removing rim. Chill.   10 servings

Variation: Spread a 10-ounce jar of Kraft cherry preserves on top of cake.

Cheesecake Germania

1 cup chocolate wafer crumbs
2 tablespoons granulated sugar
3 tablespoons Parkay margarine,
   melted
            *   *   *
3 8-ounce packages Philadelphia
   Brand cream cheese
3/4 cup granulated sugar
1/4 cup cocoa
2 teaspoons vanilla

3 eggs
            *   *   *
2 tablespoons Parkay margarine
1/4 cup evaporated milk
2 tablespoons brown sugar
1 egg, beaten
1/2 teaspoon vanilla
1/2 cup chopped pecans
1/2 cup flaked coconut

Combine crumbs, sugar and margarine; press onto bottom of 9-inch springform pan. Bake at 325°, 10 minutes. Increase oven temperature to 350°.

Combine softened cream cheese, sugar, cocoa and vanilla, mixing at medium speed on electric mixer until well blended. Add eggs, one at a time, mixing well after each addition. Pour mixture over crust. Bake at 350°, 35 minutes. Loosen cake from rim of pan; cool before removing rim. Chill.

Melt margarine in saucepan over low heat. Blend in milk, brown sugar, egg and vanilla. Cook, stirring constantly, until mixture thickens. Stir in nuts and coconut; cool. Spread on cheesecake.   10 to 12 servings

Praline "Philly" Pie

2 8-ounce packages Philadelphia
   Brand cream cheese
3/4 cup packed dark brown sugar
1 teaspoon vanilla
2 eggs

1/2 cup chopped pecans
1 9-inch graham cracker crust
Maple syrup
Pecan halves

Combine softened cream cheese, sugar and vanilla, mixing until well blended. Add eggs, one at a time, mixing well after each addition. Fold in chopped nuts. Pour into crust; bake at 325°, 35 minutes. Cool completely. Brush with syrup; top with pecan halves.   6 to 8 servings

Chocolate "Philly" Frosting

1 8-ounce package Philadelphia
   Brand cream cheese
1 tablespoon milk
1 teaspoon vanilla
Dash of salt

5 cups sifted confectioners'
   sugar
3 1-ounce squares unsweetened
   chocolate, melted

Combine softened cream cheese, milk, vanilla and salt, mixing until well blended. Add sugar, 1 cup at a time, mixing well after each addition. Stir in chocolate.   Fills and frosts two 8 or 9-inch cake layers

Cool and Creamy Cheesecake

1 cup graham cracker crumbs
1/4 cup sugar
1/4 cup Parkay margarine,
   melted

     *   *   *

1 envelope unflavored gelatin
1/4 cup cold water
1 8-ounce package Philadelphia
   Brand cream cheese

1/2 cup sugar
Dash of salt
3/4 cup milk
1/4 cup lemon juice
1 cup heavy cream, whipped
Peach slices, strawberries or
   blueberries

Combine crumbs, sugar and margarine; press onto bottom of 9-inch springform pan.

Soften gelatin in cold water; stir over low heat until dissolved. Combine softened cream cheese, sugar and salt, mixing at medium speed on electric mixer until well blended. Gradually add milk, lemon juice and gelatin; chill until slightly thickened.

Fold in whipped cream; pour over crust. Chill until firm. Remove rim of pan; top with fruit.   8 to 10 servings

Sun-Sational Cheesecake

1 cup graham cracker crumbs
3 tablespoons sugar
3 tablespoons Parkay margarine,
   melted

       *   *   *

3 8-ounce packages Philadelphia
   Brand cream cheese
1 cup sugar
3 tablespoons flour

2 tablespoons lemon juice
1 tablespoon grated lemon rind
1/2 teaspoon vanilla
4 eggs (1 separated)

                *   *   *

3/4 cup sugar
2 tablespoons cornstarch
1/2 cup water
1/4 cup lemon juice

Combine crumbs, sugar and margarine; press onto bottom of 9-inch springform pan. Bake at 325°, 10 minutes. Increase oven temperature to 450°.

Combine softened cream cheese, sugar, flour, lemon juice, rind and vanilla, mixing at medium speed on electric mixer until well blended. Add 3 eggs, one at a time, mixing well after each addition. Beat in remaining egg white; reserve yolk for glaze. Pour mixture over crust; bake at 450°, 10 minutes. Reduce oven temperature to 250°; continue baking 30 minutes. Loosen cake from rim of pan; cool before removing rim.

Combine sugar and cornstarch in saucepan; stir in water and lemon juice. Cook until clear and thickened, stirring occasionally. Add small amount to slightly beaten egg yolk; mix well. Add to hot mixture; cook 3 minutes, stirring constantly. Cool slightly. Spoon over cheesecake; chill. Garnish with lemon slices, if desired.
10 servings

Pumpkin Cheesecake

1/3 cup Parkay margarine
1/3 cup sugar
1 egg
1 1/4 cups flour

       *   *   *

2 8-ounce packages Philadelphia
   Brand cream cheese

3/4 cup sugar
1 16-ounce can pumpkin
1 teaspoon cinnamon
1/4 teaspoon ginger
1/4 teaspoon nutmeg
Dash of salt
2 eggs

Cream margarine and sugar; blend in egg. Add flour; mix well. Spread dough on bottom and 2 inches high around sides of 9-inch springform pan. Bake at 400°, 5 minutes. Reduce oven temperature to 350°.

Combine softened cream cheese and sugar, mixing at medium speed on electric mixer until well blended. Blend in pumpkin, spices and salt; mix well. Add eggs, one at a time, mixing well after each addition. Pour mixture into pastry-lined pan; smooth surface of filling to edge of crust. Bake at 350°, 50 minutes. Loosen cake from rim of pan; cool before removing rim. Chill. Garnish with whipped cream just before serving, if desired.   10 servings

Classic Cheesecake

1/3 cup Parkay margarine
1/3 cup sugar
1 egg
1 1/4 cups flour
      *   *   *
2 8-ounce packages Philadelphia
   Brand cream cheese
1/2 cup sugar
1 tablespoon lemon juice

1 teaspoon grated lemon rind
1/2 teaspoon vanilla
3 eggs
      *   *   *
1 cup dairy sour cream
1 tablespoon sugar
1 teaspoon vanilla
3/4 cup Kraft strawberry
   preserves

Cream margarine and sugar; blend in egg. Add flour; mix well. Spread dough on bottom and 1 1/2 inches high around sides of 9-inch springform pan. Bake at 450°, 5 minutes. Reduce oven temperature to 325°.

Combine softened cream cheese, sugar, lemon juice, lemon rind and vanilla, mixing at medium speed on electric mixer until well blended. Add eggs, one at a time, mixing well after each addition. Pour mixture into pastry lined pan; bake at 325°, 50 minutes.

Combine sour cream, sugar and vanilla; mix well. Spread evenly over cake; continue baking 10 minutes. Loosen cake from rim of pan; cool before removing rim. Chill. Spread with preserves.
10 servings

Peanut Butter and Jelly Cheesecake

1 cup graham cracker crumbs
3 tablespoons sugar
3 tablespoons Parkay margarine,
   melted
      *   *   *
2 8-ounce packages Philadelphia
   Brand cream cheese
1 cup sugar

1/2 cup chunk style peanut
   butter
3 tablespoons flour
4 eggs
1/2 cup milk
      *   *   *
1/2 cup Kraft concord grape jelly

Combine crumbs, sugar and margarine; press onto bottom of 9-inch springform pan. Bake at 325°, 10 minutes. Increase oven temperature to 450°.

Combine softened cream cheese, sugar, peanut butter and flour, mixing at medium speed on electric mixer until well blended. (Batter will be very stiff.) Add eggs, one at a time, mixing well after each addition. Blend in milk. Pour mixture over crust. Bake at 450°, 10 minutes. Reduce oven temperature to 250°; continue baking 40 minutes. Loosen cake from rim of pan; cool before removing rim.

Heat jelly until melted; spoon over cheesecake. Chill.
10 servings

Chocolate Cheesecake

1 cup chocolate wafer crumbs
2 tablespoons sugar
3 tablespoons Parkay margarine,
  melted

*   *   *

2 8-ounce packages Philadelphia
  Brand cream cheese
3/4 cup sugar

2 tablespoons milk
1/2 teaspoon vanilla
1 1-ounce square unsweetened
  chocolate, melted
3 eggs
Kraft chocolate flavored topping
Shredded or flaked coconut

Combine crumbs, sugar and margarine; press onto bottom of 9-inch springform pan. Bake at 325°, 10 minutes.

Combine softened cream cheese, sugar, milk and vanilla, mixing at medium speed on electric mixer until well blended. Blend in chocolate. Add eggs, one at a time, mixing well after each addition. Pour mixture over crust; bake at 325°, 40 minutes. Loosen cake from rim of pan; cool before removing rim. Chill. Garnish with topping and coconut.   10 servings

Chocolate Feather Cake

1/2 cup Parkay margarine
1 8-ounce package Philadelphia
  Brand cream cheese
1 1/4 cups sugar
1 teaspoon vanilla
2 eggs
2 cups sifted cake flour

1 teaspoon baking powder
1/2 teaspoon soda
1/4 teaspoon salt
1/2 cup milk
1 4-ounce package sweet
  chocolate, melted
Fluffy Vanilla Frosting

Combine margarine, softened cream cheese and sugar, mixing until well blended. Add vanilla and eggs; beat well. Add sifted dry ingredients to creamed mixture alternately with milk, mixing well after each addition. Blend in chocolate. Pour into two greased and floured 9-inch layer pans. Bake at 350°, 35 minutes. Cool 10 minutes; remove from pans. Cool completely. Fill and frost cake with:

Fluffy Vanilla Frosting

1/2 cup Parkay margarine
2 teaspoons vanilla
Dash of salt
1 egg white

1 tablespoon milk
4 1/2 cups sifted confectioners'
  sugar

Cream margarine; blend in vanilla and salt. Combine egg white and milk. Add sugar alternately with milk mixture, beating until light and fluffy.   Fills and frosts two 8 or 9-inch layers or frosts one 13 x 9-inch cake.

Holiday Mincemeat Pie

1 1/2 cups flour
Dash of salt
1/2 cup Parkay margarine
1 1/2 cups (6 ounces) shredded
   Kraft sharp natural cheddar
   cheese

4 to 6 tablespoons water
   *   *   *
4 cups peeled thin apple slices
1 1/2 cups mincemeat
1/3 cup chopped nuts

Combine flour and salt; cut in margarine until mixture resembles coarse crumbs. Stir in cheese. Sprinkle with water while mixing lightly with fork; form into a ball. Divide dough in half. Roll out half of dough to 11-inch circle on lightly floured surface. Place in 9-inch pie plate.

Fill pastry shell with combined apples, mincemeat and nuts. Roll out remaining dough to 11-inch circle; place over apple mixture. Seal edges of crusts; flute. Cut slits in top of pastry. Bake at 425°, 30 minutes.   6 to 8 servings

Victorian Shortcakes

2 cups flour
2 tablespoons sugar
1 tablespoon baking powder
1/2 teaspoon salt
1/3 cup shortening

1 1/2 cups (6 ounces) shredded
   Kraft sharp natural cheddar
   cheese
2/3 cup milk
Victorian Apples

Combine dry ingredients; cut in shortening until mixture resembles coarse crumbs. Stir in 1 cup cheese and milk. Roll out to 1/2-inch thickness on lightly floured surface; cut with floured 3-inch cutter. Place on greased cookie sheet; bake at 425°, 12 minutes. Cool. Split shortcakes; fill and top with Victorian Apples. Sprinkle with remaining cheese.   6 servings

Victorian Apples

Water
2 tablespoons sugar
2 1/2 cups peeled apple slices
1/4 cup raisins

1 8 1/4-ounce can crushed
   pineapple, undrained
4 teaspoons cornstarch

Combine 1/4 cup water and sugar in saucepan. Add apples and raisins; simmer until tender. Stir in pineapple. Add 1 tablespoon water to cornstarch, stirring until well blended. Add to hot fruit mixture; cook, stirring constantly, until mixture is clear and thickened. Cool slightly.

Chapter 7
Wonderful Happenings

Crêpes Parisienne

3 eggs, beaten
2/3 cup flour
1/2 teaspoon salt
1 cup milk
       *   *   *
2 cups (1/4 pound) mushroom
    slices
1/4 cup green onion slices
1/4 cup Parkay margarine

3 tablespoons flour
1/2 teaspoon salt
Dash of pepper
1 cup milk
2 1/2 cups (10 ounces) shredded
    Cracker Barrel brand sharp
    natural cheddar cheese
1 1/2 cups chopped cooked chicken

Combine eggs, flour, salt and milk; beat until smooth. Let stand 30 minutes. For each crêpe, pour 1/4 cup batter into hot, lightly greased 8-inch skillet. Cook on one side only, until underside is lightly browned.

Sauté vegetables in margarine; blend in flour and seasonings. Gradually add milk; cook, stirring constantly, until thickened. Add 1 1/2 cups cheese; stir until melted. Stir in chicken. Fill each crêpe with about 1/4 cup cheese mixture; roll up. Place seam side down in 11 3/4 x 7 1/2-inch baking dish. Bake at 350°, 20 minutes. Top with remaining cheese; continue baking until cheese melts.   4 servings

Swiss-Spinach Quiche

1 4 1/2-ounce can refrigerated
    buttermilk biscuits
1 8-ounce package Kraft natural
    Swiss cheese slices, cut into
    thin strips
2 tablespoons flour
1 cup milk

3 eggs, beaten
1/2 teaspoon salt
Dash of pepper
Dash of nutmeg
1 10-ounce package frozen
    chopped spinach, cooked,
    drained

Separate biscuit dough into six biscuits. Place in ungreased 9-inch pie plate or 9-inch quiche pan, pressing together to form crust. Toss cheese with flour. Add remaining ingredients; mix well. Pour into crust; bake at 350°, 1 hour.   8 servings

> Crêpes may be made ahead of time and refrigerated or frozen. Insert a piece of wax paper between each crêpe to keep them from sticking together and wrap carefully to prevent them from drying out. Defrost frozen crêpes before proceeding with recipe.

Opposite: Crêpes Parisienne, Swiss-Spinach Quiche

Cheese Blintzes

3 eggs, beaten
2/3 cup flour
1/2 teaspoon salt
1 cup milk

2 egg yolks
1/4 cup sugar
1 cup cottage cheese
1 teaspoon vanilla

*   *   *

1 8-ounce package Philadelphia
  Brand cream cheese

Combine eggs, flour, salt and milk; beat until smooth. Let stand 30 minutes. For each crêpe, pour about 2 tablespoons batter into hot, lightly greased 8-inch skillet. Cook on one side only, until underside is lightly browned.

Combine softened cream cheese, egg yolks and sugar, mixing until well blended. Stir in cottage cheese and vanilla. Fill each crêpe with about 2 tablespoons of mixture; roll up. Place seam side down in 11 3/4 x 7 1/2-inch baking dish. Bake at 350°, 15 to 20 minutes or until hot. Serve with Kraft strawberry preserves, if desired.

1 dozen

To make individual servings of cold soufflé, wrap a foil collar around demitasse cups and fill them with the soufflé mixture. Remove the foil just before serving.

Zesty Cheese Soufflé

3 tablespoons Parkay margarine
3 tablespoons flour
1 1/4 cups milk
1/2 teaspoon salt
Dash of pepper
1 cup (4 ounces) shredded
   Cracker Barrel brand sharp
   natural cheddar cheese

1/2 cup (2 ounces) Kraft grated
   parmesan cheese
4 eggs, separated

Make a white sauce with margarine, flour, milk and seasonings. Add cheeses; stir until melted. Remove from heat. Add small amount of mixture to slightly beaten egg yolks. Return to mixture in pan; cook, stirring constantly until cheese is melted. Cool; fold into stiffly beaten egg whites. Pour into 1 1/2-quart soufflé dish or casserole. With tip of spoon, make a slight indentation or "track" around top of soufflé, 1 inch in from edge, to form a top hat. Bake at 350°, 45 to 50 minutes or until done. Serve immediately.

6 servings

A soufflé is particularly attractive when served in a soufflé dish. But if you don't happen to have a soufflé dish on hand, bake your soufflé in a corresponding size round casserole with smooth sides.

Brandy Alexander Soufflé

2 envelopes unflavored gelatin
2 cups cold water
1 cup sugar
4 eggs, separated
1 8-ounce package Philadelphia
    Brand cream cheese

3 tablespoons crème de cacao
3 tablespoons brandy
1 cup heavy cream, whipped

Soften gelatin in 1 cup water; stir over low heat until dissolved. Add remaining water. Remove from heat; blend in 3/4 cup sugar and beaten egg yolks. Cook 3 minutes over low heat, stirring constantly. Gradually add to softened cream cheese, mixing until well blended. Stir in crème de cacao and brandy. Chill until slightly thickened. Beat egg whites until soft peaks form. Gradually add remaining sugar, beating until stiff peaks form. Fold egg whites and whipped cream into cream cheese mixture.

Wrap a 3-inch collar of aluminum foil around top of 1 1/2-quart soufflé dish; secure with tape. Pour mixture into dish; chill until firm. Remove collar before serving. Sprinkle with nutmeg and garnish with chocolate shavings, if desired.   8 to 10 servings

Top Hat Cheese Soufflé

1/3 cup Parkay margarine
1/3 cup flour
1 1/2 cups milk
1 teaspoon salt
Dash of cayenne

2 cups (8 ounces) shredded
    Cracker Barrel brand sharp
    natural cheddar cheese
6 eggs, separated

Make a white sauce with margarine, flour, milk and seasonings. Add cheese; stir until melted. Remove from heat. Add small amount of mixture to slightly beaten egg yolks. Return to mixture in pan; cook, stirring constantly, until cheese is melted. Cool; fold into stiffly beaten egg whites. Pour into 2-quart soufflé dish or casserole. With tip of spoon, make slight indentation or "track" around top of soufflé, 1 inch in from edge, to form a top hat. Bake at 300°, 1 hour and 15 minutes. Serve immediately.   6 servings

For Individual Soufflés: Pour mixture into six 2-cup soufflé dishes. Bake at 300°, 45 minutes.

Nice to know: These soufflés may be made one day in advance and frozen. Place frozen soufflé in cold oven. Bake 2-quart soufflé at 300°, 1 hour and 45 minutes. Bake individual soufflés at 300°, 1 hour.

To add flavor to a baked soufflé (cheese, meat, fish, chicken or vegetable), grease the soufflé dish and coat it with grated parmesan cheese before the soufflé mixture is added.

Grasshopper Soufflé

2 envelopes unflavored gelatin
2 cups cold water
1 cup sugar
4 eggs, separated

1 8-ounce package Philadelphia
 Brand cream cheese
1/4 cup crème de menthe
1 cup heavy cream, whipped

Soften gelatin in 1 cup water; stir over low heat until dissolved. Add remaining water; remove from heat. Blend in 3/4 cup sugar and beaten egg yolks; cook 3 minutes over low heat, stirring constantly. Gradually add to softened cream cheese, mixing until well blended. Stir in crème de menthe. Chill until slightly thickened. Beat egg whites until foamy. Gradually add remaining sugar, beating until stiff peaks form. Fold egg whites and whipped cream into cream cheese mixture.

Wrap a 3-inch collar of aluminum foil around top of 1 1/2-quart soufflé dish; secure with tape. Pour mixture into dish; chill until firm. Remove collar before serving.   8 to 10 servings

Chocolate Soufflé

2 envelopes unflavored gelatin
2 1/4 cups cold water
1 1/2 cups sugar
4 eggs, separated
3 1-ounce squares unsweetened
 chocolate, melted

1 8-ounce package Philadelphia
 Brand cream cheese
1/2 teaspoon almond extract
1 cup heavy cream, whipped

Soften gelatin in 1 cup water; stir over low heat until dissolved. Add remaining water; remove from heat. Blend in 1 cup sugar and beaten egg yolks; cook 3 minutes over low heat, stirring constantly. Add chocolate to softened cream cheese, mixing until well blended. Gradually add gelatin mixture to cream cheese mixture; mix well. Stir in extract. Chill until slightly thickened. Beat egg whites until foamy. Gradually add remaining sugar, beating until stiff peaks form. Fold egg whites and whipped cream into cream cheese mixture.

Wrap a 3-inch collar of aluminum foil around top of 1 1/2-quart soufflé dish; secure with tape. Pour mixture into dish; chill until firm. Remove collar before serving.   8 to 10 servings

Cold soufflés are an ideal dessert to serve at a buffet because they can be made ahead of time, are attractive on a buffet table, and are easy to serve.

Opposite: Grasshopper Soufflé

Parmesan Soufflé

3/4 cup (3 ounces) Kraft grated
  parmesan cheese
3 tablespoons Parkay margarine
3 tablespoons flour
3/4 cup milk
1/2 teaspoon salt

Dash of cayenne
4 eggs, separated
2 tablespoons chopped fresh
  parsley
1/2 teaspoon prepared mustard

Grease 1 1/2-quart soufflé dish or casserole; coat with 2 tablespoons cheese. Make a white sauce with margarine, flour, milk and
seasonings. Remove from heat. Add small amount of mixture to
slightly beaten egg yolks. Return to mixture in pan. Stir in 1/2 cup
cheese, parsley and mustard. Fold into stiffly beaten egg whites;
pour into soufflé dish. Top with remaining cheese. Bake at 375°, 30
to 35 minutes or until done. Serve immediately.   6 servings

Confetti Quiche

2 cups (8 ounces) shredded Kraft
  sharp natural cheddar cheese
2 tablespoons flour
4 eggs, slightly beaten
1 1/2 cups milk

1/4 cup green onion slices
2 tablespoons chopped pimiento
1/4 teaspoon salt
Dash of pepper
1 9-inch unbaked pastry shell

Toss cheese with flour. Add eggs, milk, onion, pimiento and
seasonings; mix well. Pour into pastry shell; bake at 350°, 1 hour or
until set.   6 servings

Quiche Olé

2 cups (8 ounces) shredded Kraft
  sharp natural cheddar cheese
1/4 cup flour
4 eggs, slightly beaten
1 1/2 cups milk

1/2 teaspoon salt
Dash of cayenne
1 9-inch unbaked pastry shell
Spanish Sauce

Toss cheese with flour. Add eggs, milk and seasonings; mix well.
Pour into pastry shell; bake at 350°, 1 hour. Cut into wedges; top
with:

Spanish Sauce

1/2 cup chopped green pepper
1/2 cup celery slices

1/4 cup chopped onion
1 cup catsup or chili sauce

Heat vegetables in catsup until crisp-tender.   1 1/2 cups
4 to 6 servings

Cheddar-Tuna Quiche

1 1/2 cups cooked rice
1 egg, slightly beaten
     *   *   *
2 cups (8 ounces) shredded Kraft
   sharp natural cheddar cheese
2 tablespoons flour
3 eggs, beaten

1 cup milk
1 6 1/2-ounce can tuna, drained,
   flaked
1/3 cup celery slices
1/2 teaspoon salt
Dash of pepper
8 tomato wedges

Combine rice and egg; mix well. Pour mixture into greased 9-inch pie plate, pressing to form a crust.

Toss cheese with flour. Add eggs, milk, tuna, celery and seasonings; mix well. Pour into crust. Bake at 350°, 1 hour. Garnish with tomato wedges.   8 servings

Quiche Lorraine

2 cups (8 ounces) shredded Kraft
   natural Swiss cheese
2 tablespoons flour
1 1/2 cups half and half
4 eggs, slightly beaten

8 crisply cooked bacon slices,
   crumbled
1/2 teaspoon salt
Dash of pepper
1 9-inch unbaked pastry shell

Toss cheese with flour. Add half and half, eggs, bacon and seasonings; mix well. Pour into pastry shell and bake at 350°, 40 to 45 minutes or until set.   6 servings

Variation: Substitute 3/4 cup chopped ham for bacon.

Quiche, cut into very small portions, makes a flavorful hot appetizer.

Cheese Fondue Surprise

1 3/4 cups milk
3 cups French bread cubes
2 cups (8 ounces) shredded Kraft
   sharp natural cheddar cheese

1 teaspoon salt
1/2 teaspoon dry mustard
Dash of pepper
4 eggs, separated

Heat milk. Add remaining ingredients except eggs; stir until cheese melts. Remove from heat. Gradually add slightly beaten egg yolks; cool. Fold into stiffly beaten egg whites; pour into 2-quart casserole. Bake at 325°, 50 to 55 minutes or until set. Serve immediately. 6 to 8 servings

Quiche makes an excellent, easy-to-make main course for brunch.

Alpine Fondue

1 6-ounce package Kraft shredded
   natural Swiss cheese
1 tablespoon flour
1 garlic clove, cut in half

3/4 cup dry white wine
Salt and pepper
1 tablespoon Kirsch
French or Vienna bread chunks

Toss cheese and flour together. Rub inside of fondue pot or chafing dish with garlic. Pour in wine; heat until bubbles rise to surface (never let it boil). Add cheese mixture, 1/2 cup at a time. Stir constantly, letting cheese melt completely before adding more. Continue stirring until mixture bubbles lightly. Stir in seasonings and Kirsch. Keep fondue bubbling gently while serving. If it becomes too thick, pour in a little warmed wine. Serve with bread.
3 to 4 servings

Cheese 'n Ham Fondue

2 tablespoons chopped onion
1 tablespoon Parkay margarine
3 eggs, beaten
3/4 cup milk
1/2 teaspoon salt
1/4 teaspoon dry mustard

3 cups soft bread cubes
1 cup chopped ham
1/4 pound Old English sharp
   pasteurized process American
   cheese, cubed

Sauté onion in margarine. Combine eggs, milk and seasonings; stir in remaining ingredients. Let stand 15 minutes; pour into 1-quart casserole. Bake at 350°, 50 minutes.   4 servings

Fall Fondue

1 16-ounce jar Cheez Whiz
   pasteurized process cheese
   spread
1/2 cup Parkay margarine
1 8 3/4-ounce can whole
   kernel corn, drained

1/4 cup chopped pimiento
2 tablespoons chopped green
   chili pepper
French bread chunks

Heat process cheese spread and margarine over low heat in fondue pot or saucepan, stirring occasionally, until process cheese spread melts. Stir in corn, pimiento and pepper. Serve hot with bread.
2 1/2 cups

Fondue not only makes a great appetizer, but can also be served as a main course at an informal supper. Serve with a crisp tossed salad and dessert.

Backyard Fondue

2 cups (8 ounces) shredded Casino
   brand natural muenster cheese
2 tablespoons flour
1 cup beer

1/2 teaspoon prepared mustard
French or Vienna bread, cut
   into chunks, or frankfurters,
   cut into 1-inch pieces

Toss together cheese and flour. Heat beer in fondue pot or sauce-pan until bubbles rise to surface (never let it boil). Add cheese mixture, 1/2 cup at a time. Stir constantly, letting cheese melt completely before adding more. Continue stirring until mixture bubbles lightly. Stir in mustard. Serve with bread or frankfurters.   2 cups

Impromptu Fondue

1 16-ounce jar Cheez Whiz
   pasteurized process cheese
   spread

1/2 cup Parkay margarine
French bread chunks

Heat process cheese spread and margarine over low heat in fondue pot or saucepan, stirring occasionally, until process cheese spread melts. Serve hot with bread.   2 cups

Variations: Stir in 1/2 cup chopped tomato and 2 tablespoons chopped onion.   2 1/2 cups
      Substitute two 8-ounce jars Cheez Whiz with pimento for Cheez Whiz. Stir in a 6 1/2-ounce can tuna, drained, flaked and 1/4 cup chopped green pepper.   3 cups
      Substitute two 8-ounce jars Cheez Whiz with jalapeño peppers for Cheez Whiz. Add 1 cup chopped tomato.   2 1/2 cups
      Stir in 2 tablespoons chopped pimiento, 2 tablespoons chopped green pepper and 2 tablespoons chopped onion.   2 cups
      Stir in a 4-ounce can Vienna sausage, drained, chopped and a 2 1/2-ounce jar mushrooms, drained.   3 cups

Hearty Half-Time Fondue

1 5-ounce jar Kraft pasteurized
   neufchatel cheese spread with
   relish
1 5-ounce jar Old English sharp
   pasteurized process cheese
   spread

1 tablespoon milk
Corn chips
French bread chunks

Heat process cheese spreads and milk over low heat, stirring until smooth. Serve warm with corn chips and bread chunks.
1 1/2 cups

Crêpes Florentine

3 eggs, beaten
2/3 cup flour
1/2 teaspoon salt
1 cup milk

*   *   *

1/4 cup Parkay margarine
1/4 cup flour
1 1/4 cups milk
1/2 teaspoon salt

3/4 cup (3 ounces) Kraft grated
    parmesan cheese
1 10-ounce package frozen
    chopped spinach, cooked,
    drained
1 cup (4 ounces) Kraft shredded
    natural Swiss cheese
1 4-ounce can mushrooms, drained

Combine eggs, flour, salt and milk; beat until smooth. Let stand 30 minutes. For each crêpe, pour 1/4 cup batter into hot, lightly greased 8-inch skillet. Cook on one side only, until underside is lightly browned.

Make a white sauce with margarine, flour, milk and salt. Add parmesan cheese; stir until melted. Combine spinach, Swiss cheese, mushrooms and 1 cup cheese sauce. Fill each crêpe with about 1/4 cup spinach mixture; roll up. Place seam side down in 11 3/4 x 7 1/2-inch baking dish. Top with remaining cheese sauce. Sprinkle with paprika, if desired. Bake at 350°, 25 to 30 minutes or until hot.   4 servings

Crêpes Marquis

3 eggs, beaten
2/3 cup flour
1/2 teaspoon salt
1 cup milk

*   *   *

8 bacon slices
1/2 cup chopped onion

1/2 cup chopped green pepper
2 cups (8 ounces) shredded
    Cracker Barrel brand sharp
    natural cheddar cheese
1 2 1/2-ounce jar sliced
    mushrooms, drained
1 8-ounce can tomato sauce

Combine eggs, flour, salt and milk; beat until smooth. Let stand 30 minutes. For each crêpe, pour 1/4 cup batter into hot, lightly greased 8-inch skillet. Cook on one side only, until underside is lightly browned.

Fry bacon until crisp; remove from skillet. Drain fat, reserving 2 tablespoons. Cook onion and green pepper in bacon fat until tender. Crumble bacon. Combine bacon, onion, green pepper, 1 1/2 cups cheese and mushrooms; mix lightly. Fill each crêpe with about 1/4 cup cheese mixture; roll up. Place seam side down in 11 3/4 x 7 1/2-inch baking dish; top with tomato sauce. Bake at 350°, 15 minutes. Top with remaining cheese; continue baking until cheese melts.   4 servings

Crêpes à l'Orange

4 eggs, beaten
1 cup flour
1 cup milk
2 tablespoons Parkay margarine,
    melted
1/2 teaspoon salt

*   *   *

1 8-ounce package Philadephia
    Brand cream cheese

1/4 cup Parkay margarine, melted
1/2 cup Kraft marshmallow creme
1 cup sifted confectioners' sugar
1/4 teaspoon almond extract
1/2 cup chopped almonds
Orange Sauce

Combine eggs, flour, milk, margarine and salt, beating until smooth. Let stand 30 minutes. For each crêpe, pour about 2 tablespoons batter into hot, lightly greased 8-inch skillet. Cook on one side only, until underside is lightly browned.

Combine softened cream cheese and margarine; mix well. Stir in marshmallow creme. Add sugar and extract; mix well. Fold in nuts. Fill each crêpe with about 3 tablespoons cream cheese mixture; roll up. Top with:

Orange Sauce

1 cup Kraft pure 100%
    pasteurized orange juice
2 tablespoons cornstarch

1/4 cup brandy
1 11-ounce can mandarin
    orange segments, drained

In saucepan, gradually add juice to cornstarch, stirring until well blended. Stir in brandy. Cook over medium heat until clear and thickened; stir in oranges.   2 cups   8 servings

---

Leftover crêpes may be cut into small pieces, deep-fried, and tossed with grated parmesan cheese. Serve as an appetizer or with soup or salad.

"Philly" Brunch Quiche

1 10-inch unbaked pastry shell
1 cup milk
1 8-ounce package Philadelphia
   Brand cream cheese, cubed
1/4 cup chopped onion
1 tablespoon Parkay margarine

4 eggs, beaten
1 cup finely chopped ham
1/4 cup chopped pimiento
1/4 teaspoon dill weed
Dash of pepper

Bake pastry shell at 400°, 12 to 15 minutes or until lightly browned. Cool. Reduce oven temperature to 350°. Heat milk and cream cheese over low heat, stirring occasionally. Sauté onion in margarine. Gradually add cheese sauce to eggs; stir in onion and remaining ingredients. Pour into pastry shell; bake at 350°, 35 to 40 minutes or until set. Garnish with parsley and pimiento, if desired.   8 servings

Opposite: Toasty Biscuit Loaf (page 120), Hearty Corn Bread (page 120)

Toasty Biscuit Loaf

2 10-ounce cans refrigerated
   buttermilk flaky biscuits
1/4 cup Parkay margarine, melted

1/2 cup (2 ounces) Kraft grated
   parmesan cheese
2 teaspoons sesame seeds,
   toasted

Dip one side of biscuits in margarine and then in cheese. Place eight
biscuits, cheese side up, in bottom of greased 9 x 5-inch loaf pan.
Overlap remaining biscuits to cover top. Sprinkle with sesame
seeds; bake at 375°, 40 minutes.   1 loaf

Hearty Corn Bread

1 cup cornmeal
1 cup flour
1 tablespoon baking powder
1 teaspoon salt
2 cups (8 ounces) shredded
   Casino brand natural
   monterey jack cheese

1 cup milk
1/4 cup Squeeze Parkay margarine
1 egg, beaten
1 green pepper, cut into rings

Combine dry ingredients; stir in 1 cup cheese. Add combined milk,
margarine and egg; mix until blended. Pour into greased 9-inch
layer pan. Cover with remaining cheese; top with green pepper.
Bake at 425°, 20 minutes.   6 to 8 servings

It's fun to make and serve miniature bread loaves, and you don't
need special pans. Just divide a 9 x 5-inch loaf pan into four sections with strips of heavy foil. Instead of one large loaf, you'll have
four miniature loaves.

Cheyenne Cheese Bread

6 bacon slices
3 3/4 cups flour
5 teaspoons baking powder
1 teaspoon salt

2 cups (8 ounces) shredded
   Kraft natural Swiss cheese
1/4 cup chopped onion
1 1/2 cups milk
2 eggs, slightly beaten

Fry bacon until crisp; remove from skillet. Drain fat, reserving 2
tablespoons. Combine dry ingredients. Crumble bacon; add bacon,
cheese and onion to dry ingredients. Combine reserved bacon fat,
milk and eggs; add to cheese mixture, mixing until just moistened.
Spoon into greased 9 x 5-inch loaf pan. Bake at 375°, 1 hour.
Remove from pan immediately.   1 loaf

Cheddar Oatmeal Bread

1 package active dry yeast
1/2 cup warm water
1 cup old fashioned or
  quick oats, uncooked
1/2 cup milk, scalded
1/2 cup hot water

1 8-ounce package Kraft
  sharp natural cheddar
  cheese, shredded
2 tablespoons sugar
2 teaspoons salt
3 cups flour

Soften yeast in warm water. Combine oats, milk and hot water; cool to lukewarm. Stir in softened yeast, cheese, sugar and salt. Stir in 2 1/2 cups flour; mix well. Knead 3 to 5 minutes, working in remaining flour. Place dough in lightly greased bowl, turning once to grease surface. Cover and let rise in warm place until double in bulk, about 1 hour. Punch down. Turn out on lightly floured surface; shape into loaf. Place in well greased 9 x 5-inch loaf pan. Cover and let rise in warm place 30 minutes. Bake at 350°, 45 to 50 minutes or until deep golden brown. Remove from pan immediately. 1 loaf

Alpine Caraway Quick Bread

3 1/2 cups flour
5 teaspoons baking powder
1/2 teaspoon salt
1/3 cup Parkay margarine
2 cups (8 ounces) shredded
  Kraft natural Swiss cheese

1 teaspoon caraway seeds
1 1/2 cups milk
2 eggs, slightly beaten
2 teaspoons prepared mustard

Combine dry ingredients. Cut in margarine until mixture resembles coarse crumbs; stir in cheese and caraway seeds. Combine milk, eggs and mustard; add to cheese mixture, mixing until just moistened. Pour into greased 9 x 5-inch loaf pan. Bake at 375°, 1 hour and 15 minutes. Remove from pan immediately. 1 loaf

Parmesan Flat Bread

3 cups flour
1 tablespoon baking powder
1 teaspoon sage
1/2 teaspoon salt
1 1/2 cups milk

2/3 cup Parkay margarine,
  melted
1/2 cup (2 ounces) Kraft
  grated parmesan cheese

Combine dry ingredients. Mix milk and 1/3 cup margarine; add to flour mixture, mixing until just moistened. Spread into greased 13 x 9-inch baking pan. Brush with remaining margarine; sprinkle with cheese. Bake at 400°, 25 to 30 minutes or until top is crisp and golden brown. Cut into rectangles; serve warm. 6 to 8 servings

Quick Cheese Bread

3 3/4 cups flour
5 teaspoons baking powder
1/2 teaspoon salt
1/3 cup Parkay margarine

2 1/2 cups (10 ounces) shredded
   Kraft sharp natural cheddar
   cheese
1 1/2 cups milk
2 eggs, slightly beaten

Combine dry ingredients. Cut margarine into flour until mixture resembles coarse crumbs; stir in cheese. Combine milk and eggs; add to cheese mixture, mixing until just moistened. Spoon into greased 9 x 5-inch loaf pan. Bake at 375°, 1 hour. Remove from pan immediately.   1 loaf

Variation: Add 1/2 teaspoon of dill weed to dry ingredients.

To make cheese flavored croutons, toss a cup of bread cubes with 2 tablespoons of melted margarine and 1 tablespoon of grated parmesan cheese. Bake at 400°, 5 minutes. Cheese flavored croutons are great in salads, with soup or atop a casserole.

Apple Brunch Coffee Cake

1 8-ounce package Philadelphia
   Brand cream cheese
1/2 cup Parkay margarine
1 1/4 cups granulated sugar
2 eggs
1 teaspoon vanilla
1 3/4 cups flour
1 teaspoon baking powder
1/2 teaspoon soda

1/4 teaspoon salt
1/4 cup milk
3 cups peeled thin apple
   slices

        *   *   *

1/2 cup packed brown sugar
1/2 cup flour
1/4 cup Parkay margarine
1/2 teaspoon cinnamon

Combine softened cream cheese, margarine and sugar, mixing until well blended. Add eggs and vanilla; beat well. Add combined dry ingredients to creamed mixture, alternately with milk, mixing well after each addition. Pour into greased and floured 13 x 9-inch baking pan. Top with apples.

   Combine brown sugar, flour, margarine and cinnamon. Sprinkle over apples. Bake at 350°, 45 to 50 minutes or until wooden pick inserted in center comes out clean.   8 to 10 servings

Opposite: Quick Cheese Bread

Cheesy Corn Bread

1 cup flour
1 cup cornmeal
2 tablespoons sugar
1 tablespoon baking powder
1 teaspoon salt
1/4 teaspoon dry mustard

2 cups (8 ounces) shredded Kraft
   sharp natural cheddar cheese
1 egg, slightly beaten
1 cup milk
1/4 cup all purpose oil

Combine dry ingredients; stir in cheese. Combine egg, milk and oil; add to cheese mixture, mixing until just moistened. Pour into greased 9-inch square pan. Bake at 425°, 20 minutes. Cut into squares; serve warm.   6 to 8 servings

Variation: Bake in greased 1 1/2-quart ring mold.

Cheddar Squares

2 cups flour
1 tablespoon baking powder
1 teaspoon salt
1/3 cup Parkay margarine
1 cup (4 ounces) shredded Kraft
   sharp natural cheddar cheese

1/2 cup chopped onion
2 tablespoons chopped pimiento
2/3 cup milk

Combine dry ingredients. Cut in margarine until mixture resembles coarse crumbs. Add cheese, onion and pimiento; mix well. Add milk, mixing until just moistened. Spread dough into greased 9-inch square pan. Bake at 450°, 25 to 30 minutes or until wooden pick inserted in center comes out clean. Cut into squares; serve warm. 6 to 8 servings

---

Cheese bread loaves, like the Alpine Caraway Quick Bread and Quick Cheese Bread included in this chapter, are particularly good when toasted to bring out the cheese flavor.

Bayou Drop Biscuits

2 cups flour
2 teaspoons baking powder
3 tablespoons Parkay margarine

1 8-ounce jar Cheez Whiz
   pasteurized process cheese
   spread
1/3 cup milk

Combine dry ingredients; cut in margarine until mixture resembles coarse crumbs. Add process cheese spread and milk; mix well. Drop by rounded tablespoonfuls onto greased cookie sheet. Bake at 450°, 8 to 10 minutes or until golden brown.   1 dozen

Cheesy Skillet Biscuits

Kraft sharp natural cheddar
  cheese
2 cups flour
1 tablespoon baking powder

1 teaspoon salt
2 tablespoons freeze-dried chives
3/4 cup milk
1/4 cup Parkay margarine, melted

Cut six ounces of cheese into eight 2 x 1 x 1/2-inch slices. Combine dry ingredients; stir in chives. Add milk and margarine, mixing until just moistened. Knead dough about ten times on lightly floured surface. Pat dough out to 12 x 9-inch rectangle; place cheese slices, equally spaced, on half the dough. Fold other half of dough over cheese; cut into 3 x 2-inch rectangles. Press edges of dough together to seal. Place in generously greased, hot 12-inch skillet. Cover; cook over low heat 10 minutes. Turn; cover and continue cooking 5 minutes or until golden brown.   8 biscuits

---

Add shredded cheddar cheese to your favorite biscuit recipe for special, extra flavor. Toss the cheese with dry ingredients before adding the liquid.

Tempting Long Loaf

1/4 cup chopped onion
1/4 cup chopped green pepper
1/2 cup soft Parkay margarine
1 Vienna bread loaf

1 cup (4 ounces) Kraft shredded
  natural low moisture part-skim
  mozzarella cheese
1 tablespoon chopped pimiento

Sauté onion and green pepper in 1 tablespoon margarine. Cut bread in half lengthwise; cut each half crosswise in 1 1/2-inch slices to within 1/2 inch of bottom crust. Combine onion, green pepper, cheese, remaining margarine and pimiento; mix well. Spread on bread halves. Wrap each half in aluminum foil. Bake at 375°, 15 minutes.

Cheezy Muffins

1 8-ounce jar Cheez Whiz
  pasteurized process cheese
  spread
1/3 cup Parkay margarine
1/4 cup milk

1 egg, slightly beaten
2 cups flour
1/4 cup sugar
1 tablespoon baking powder
1/4 teaspoon salt

Heat process cheese spread, margarine and milk over low heat; stir until sauce is smooth. Remove from heat; blend in egg. Add to combined dry ingredients, mixing until just moistened. Spoon into well greased medium size muffin pan, filling each cup half full. Bake at 400°, 15 minutes.   1 1/2 dozen

Parmesan Twists

1 8-ounce can refrigerated   Kraft grated parmesan cheese
crescent dinner rolls

Separate crescent dough into four rectangles. Sprinkle both sides of each rectangle with cheese. Roll rectangles on an unfloured surface to 7 x 4-inch rectangles; cut each rectangle into six lengthwise strips. Twist strips; place on greased cookie sheet. Bake at 375°, 7 to 10 minutes or until lightly browned.   24 twists

Variation: To make appetizer twists, cut each strip in half before twisting.

Nice to know: For crisper twists, bake a day in advance and store in loosely covered container.

Remember, cheese bread or biscuits are great bases for creamed main dishes. Spoon creamed chicken, eggs or tuna over toasted slices of cheese bread or opened hot cheese biscuits.

Opposite: Club of Your Choice (page 128), Southwestern Sloppy Joes (page 128),
Crunchy Toastwiches (page 128)

Chapter 9
**Sandwiches
to Remember**

Club of Your Choice

Rye bread slices
Miracle Whip salad dressing
Lettuce

Kraft American Singles
  pasteurized process cheese food
Tomato slices
Crisply cooked bacon slices

For each sandwich, spread one slice of bread with salad dressing; cover with lettuce, process cheese food, tomato, bacon and second slice of bread. Top with process cheese food, tomato, bacon and third slice of bread, spread with salad dressing. Cut into quarters.

Southwestern Sloppy Joes

1/2 pound ground beef
1 18-ounce jar baked beans
1/2 cup Kraft barbecue sauce
1/4 cup chopped onion
1/4 cup chopped green pepper

Corn bread, cut into 3-inch
  squares
Kraft mild natural colby cheese
  slices, cut into triangles

Brown meat; drain. Add beans, barbecue sauce, onion and green pepper. Cover; simmer 15 minutes. For each sandwich, split corn bread; top with cheese. Broil until cheese melts; spoon meat mixture over cheese. Top with additional cheese, if desired.
6 to 8 servings

Crunchy Toastwiches

2 eggs, slightly beaten
1/2 cup milk
16 white bread slices

Kraft American Singles
  pasteurized process cheese food
1 1/2 cups crushed corn chips

Combine eggs and milk. For each sandwich, cover slice of bread with process cheese food; top with second slice of bread. Dip in egg mixture, then in corn chips, turning to coat both sides. Bake at 350°, 5 minutes. Turn sandwiches; continue baking 5 minutes or until process cheese food melts.   8 sandwiches

Heidelburger Grill

Rye bread slices
Kraft natural Swiss cheese
  slices

Hot broiled beef patties
Onion slices, sautéed
Soft Parkay margarine

For each sandwich, cover one slice of bread with cheese, patty, onion, cheese and second slice of bread. Spread bread with margarine; grill on both sides until lightly browned.

Tacoburgers

1 pound ground beef
1 cup crushed corn chips
1/4 cup chili sauce
Kraft American Singles
   pasteurized process cheese food

5 poppy seed buns, split
Chopped tomato
Chopped avocado

Combine meat, corn chips and chili sauce. Shape into five patties. Broil or grill on both sides to desired doneness. Top with process cheese food; heat until process cheese food melts. For each sandwich, cover bottom half of bun with patty, tomato and avocado. Serve with top half of bun.   5 sandwiches

Pizzaburgers

1 1/2 pounds ground beef
1/2 teaspoon garlic salt
1/4 teaspoon pepper
        *   *   *
1 16-ounce can tomatoes,
   drained, chopped
1 8-ounce can tomato sauce
1 4-ounce can mushrooms, drained

1 teaspoon oregano
3 individual French bread
   loaves, baked, split
1 8-ounce package Kraft natural
   low moisture part-skim
   mozzarella cheese slices
2 cups onion rings, sautéed

Combine meat and seasonings; mix lightly. Shape into 6 oval patties; broil on both sides to desired doneness.
   Combine tomatoes, tomato sauce, mushrooms and oregano; simmer 15 minutes. For each sandwich, top bread half with patty; spread with sauce. Top with cheese, onion and additional sauce. Broil until cheese melts.   6 sandwiches

Pizza Pockets

1 pound ground beef
1/4 cup chopped onion
1/4 cup chopped green pepper
2 cups (8 ounces) shredded Kraft
   sharp natural cheddar cheese
1 6-ounce can tomato paste

1/2 teaspoon salt
1/2 teaspoon garlic salt
1/2 teaspoon oregano
2 8-ounce cans refrigerated
   crescent dinner rolls

Brown meat; drain. Add onion and green pepper; cook until tender. Add cheese, tomato paste and seasonings; mix well. Separate each can of crescent dough into four rectangles; place on ungreased cookie sheet. Press perforations to seal. Spoon 1/3 cup of meat mixture onto each rectangle. Fold dough over filling; press edges to seal. Bake at 375°, 20 minutes.   8 servings

Festival Sandwich Loaf

1 1 1/2-pound unsliced sandwich
   loaf, crusts trimmed
Liver Sausage Spread
Golden Spread

Deviled Ham Spread
2 8-ounce packages Philadelphia
   Brand cream cheese
1/4 cup milk

Cut bread into four lengthwise slices. Spread one slice of bread with Liver Sausage Spread; cover with second slice of bread, spread with Golden Spread. Top with third slice of bread, spread with Deviled Ham Spread and cover with fourth slice of bread. Combine softened cream cheese and milk, mixing until well blended. Frost sandwich loaf.   12 servings

Liver Sausage Spread

1/4 pound liver sausage
1 tablespoon Miracle Whip
   salad dressing

1 tablespoon chopped onion

Combine all ingredients; mix well.

Golden Spread

2 5-ounce jars Old English
   sharp pasteurized process
   cheese spread

2 tablespoons milk
2 tablespoons chopped fresh
   parsley

Combine all ingredients; mix well.

Deviled Ham Spread

2 2 1/4-ounce cans deviled ham

1 tablespoon sweet pickle relish

Combine ingredients; mix well.

Sloppy Joe Grills

1/2 pound ground beef
1/2 cup Kraft barbecue sauce
1/4 cup water
2 tablespoons chopped green
   pepper

2 tablespoons chopped onion
16 white bread slices
Kraft American Singles
   pasteurized process cheese food
Soft Parkay margarine

Brown meat; drain. Add barbecue sauce, water, green pepper and onion. Simmer 15 minutes. For each sandwich, spread slice of bread with 2 tablespoons of meat mixture. Top with process cheese food and second slice of bread. Spread bread with margarine. Place sandwiches on cookie sheet; broil on each side until golden brown.   8 sandwiches

Meatball Cheddarwiches

1 pound ground beef
1 teaspoon salt
1 tablespoon all purpose oil
2 tablespoons flour

1 cup water
Italian bread slices
Kraft sharp natural cheddar
   cheese slices

Combine meat and salt; mix lightly. Shape into 1-inch meatballs. Brown in oil. Remove meatballs from oil; add flour. Cook over medium heat until flour is brown, stirring constantly. Add water; bring to a boil. Add meatballs; continue cooking 3 to 5 minutes or until sauce thickens. For each sandwich, cover slice of bread with cheese; broil until cheese melts. Spoon meatballs and sauce over cheese.   4 to 6 servings

Monterey Barbecue Sandwiches

1 pound ground beef
1/2 cup chopped onion
1 16-ounce can kidney beans,
   drained
1/2 cup Kraft barbecue sauce
1 teaspoon chili powder

1/2 cup Cheez Whiz pasteurized
   process cheese spread or
   Cheez Whiz with jalapeño
   peppers
6 hamburger buns, split,
   toasted

Brown meat; drain. Add onion; cook until tender. Stir in beans, barbecue sauce and chili powder. Cover; simmer 20 minutes. Add process cheese spread; stir until melted. For each sandwich, cover bottom half of bun with meat mixture and top half of bun. 6 sandwiches

---

Thinly sliced sandwich ingredients are easy to handle and easy to eat.

Southwestern Tacos

1 pound ground beef
3/4 cup Kraft barbecue sauce
1/4 cup water
1/4 cup chopped onion
2 teaspoons chili powder
1/4 teaspoon salt
Dash of pepper

10 taco shells
Cheez Whiz pasteurized process
   cheese spread with jalapeño
   peppers
1 1/2 cups shredded lettuce
3/4 cup chopped tomato

Brown meat; drain. Stir in barbecue sauce, water, onion and seasonings. Simmer 15 minutes. For each taco, spread inside of taco with cheese spread; fill with meat mixture, lettuce and tomato.   10 tacos

Doggie-Burgers

1 pound ground beef
1 teaspoon salt
1/4 teaspoon pepper
3 frankfurters, cut in half
  lengthwise
Kraft barbecue sauce

Deluxe Choice American
  pasteurized process cheese,
  cut into triangles
6 frankfurter buns, split
Prepared mustard
Dill pickle slices

Combine beef and seasonings; mix lightly. Form beef around half of frankfurter to fit frankfurter bun. Brush with barbecue sauce; broil to desired doneness. Top with cheese; return to broiler until cheese begins to melt. For each sandwich, spread bottom half of bun with mustard. Cover with pickle slices, meat and top half of bun.
6 sandwiches

Party Sloppy Joes

1/2 pound ground beef
1/4 cup chopped onion
1/2 pound frankfurters, sliced
3/4 cup Kraft barbecue sauce

1/4 cup sweet pickle relish
8 hamburger buns, split
Velveeta pasteurized process
  cheese spread, sliced

Brown beef; drain. Add onion; cook until tender. Add frankfurters, barbecue sauce and pickle relish. Cover; simmer 15 minutes. For each sandwich, cover bottom half of bun with process cheese spread; top with meat mixture. Serve with top half of bun.
8 sandwiches

For maximum flavor and good texture, frozen sandwiches should not be stored in the freezer longer than 1 month. Thaw them in the freezer wrap at room temperature 2 to 4 hours, or in the refrigerator 5 to 6 hours.

Denver Delight Sandwiches

2 tablespoons chopped green
  pepper
1 tablespoon chopped onion
2 tablespoons Parkay margarine
6 eggs, beaten
1/2 cup chopped cooked ham

1/3 cup milk
Salt and pepper
6 hamburger buns, split,
  toasted
Velveeta pasteurized process
  cheese spread, sliced

Sauté green pepper and onion in margarine. Add combined eggs, ham, milk and seasonings. Cook over low heat, stirring occasionally, until eggs are cooked. For each sandwich, cover bottom half of bun with process cheese spread; broil until process cheese spread melts. Top with scrambled eggs; serve with top half of bun.
6 sandwiches

Waffled American Sandwich

White bread slices
Boiled ham slices
Thin apple slices

Kraft American Singles
   pasteurized process cheese food
Parkay margarine

For each sandwich, cover slice of bread with ham, apples and process cheese food; top with second slice of bread. Spread bread with margarine; grill in hot waffle iron until lightly browned.

Ham and Egg Grills

4 hard-cooked eggs, chopped
2/3 cup chopped cooked ham
1/2 cup chopped celery
Kraft real mayonnaise

16 white bread slices
Kraft pimento Singles
   pasteurized process cheese food
Parkay margarine

Combine eggs, ham, celery and enough mayonnaise to moisten; mix lightly. For each sandwich, cover slice of bread with egg mixture, process cheese food and second slice of bread. Spread bread with margarine; grill on both sides until lightly browned.
8 sandwiches

Waldorf Sandwiches

1/2 cup chopped cooked ham
1/2 cup chopped apple
1/2 cup celery slices
1/4 cup raisins
1/4 cup chopped walnuts

Miracle Whip salad dressing
8 whole wheat bread slices
Kraft American Singles
   pasteurized process cheese food

Combine ham, apple, celery, raisins, nuts and enough salad dressing to moisten; mix lightly. For each sandwich, cover slice of bread with ham mixture, process cheese food and second slice of bread.   4 sandwiches

Crispy Ham 'n Swiss Sandwiches

12 white bread slices
Soft Parkay margarine
Prepared mustard
6 Kraft natural Swiss cheese
  slices, cut in half

6 boiled ham slices
6 tomato slices
2 eggs, beaten
2 tablespoons milk
1 cup corn flake crumbs

For each sandwich, spread two slices of bread lightly with margarine and mustard. Cover one slice of bread with cheese, ham, tomato and second slice of bread. Dip into combined egg and milk mixture, then into corn flake crumbs. Melt 1 tablespoon margarine in skillet; grill on both sides until golden brown.   6 sandwiches

Savory Hero

1 pound ground beef
1 6-ounce can tomato paste
2 tablespoons chopped onion
1 teaspoon salt
Dash of pepper
1 Vienna bread loaf, cut
   in half lengthwise

Kraft American Singles
   pasteurized process cheese food
Tomato slices
Green pepper rings

Combine meat, tomato paste, onion and seasonings; mix lightly.
Spread half of meat mixture on each half of bread. Place on
ungreased cookie sheet; bake at 450°, 20 minutes. Top with layers
of process cheese food, tomato and green pepper. Continue baking
until process cheese food melts.   8 servings

Variations: Add 1/2 teaspoon oregano and 1/4 teaspoon garlic
powder to meat mixture.
         Add 1 tablespoon chili powder to meat mixture.

To store sandwiches properly, wrap them individually in moisture-
vapor-proof wrap. This will prevent transfer of flavors and will also
prevent the sandwiches from drying out. Eat sandwiches within 4
hours after they have been removed from the refrigerator or while
still cool.

Meal Pleasing Burgers

2 pounds ground beef
1/2 cup chopped onion
1 cup soft bread crumbs
1/3 cup Kraft barbecue sauce
1 egg
1 1/4 teaspoons salt

Kraft American Singles
   pasteurized process cheese food
8 tomato slices
Pickle chips
8 white bread slices, toasted

Combine meat, onion, bread crumbs, barbecue sauce, egg and salt;
mix lightly. Place meat mixture in 15 1/2 x 10 1/2-inch jelly roll pan;
press mixture evenly to within 1 inch of edge of pan. Bake at 350°,
20 minutes; drain. Top meat mixture with eight process cheese
food slices and tomato slices; continue baking until process cheese
food melts. Cut into squares; garnish with pickle chips. Serve on
toast.   8 sandwiches

Opposite: Savory Hero

Hearty Bean Burgers

1/2 pound ground beef
1/4 cup chopped onion
1/4 cup chopped green pepper
1 18-ounce jar baked beans
1/2 cup Cheez Whiz pasteurized
  process cheese spread or
  Cheez Whiz with jalapeño
  peppers

Prepared mustard
3 hamburger buns, split,
  toasted

Brown meat; drain. Add onion and green pepper; cook until tender.
Stir in beans and process cheese spread; heat. For each sandwich,
spread half of bun with mustard; top with meat mixture.
6 servings

Harvest Time Sandwich

Whole wheat bread slices
Kraft real mayonnaise
Lettuce

Spiced apple rings
Kraft natural brick cheese slices
Cooked pork slices

For each sandwich, spread slice of bread with mayonnaise. Cover
with lettuce, apple rings, cheese, pork and second slice of bread.

Smorgasbord Sandwich

Rye bread slices
Prepared mustard
Lettuce
Kraft natural caraway cheese
  slices, cut into triangles

Roast beef slices, rolled
Tomato slices, cut in half
Hard-cooked egg slices
Paprika

For each sandwich, spread slice of bread with mustard. Top with
lettuce, cheese, meat, tomato and eggs. Sprinkle eggs with paprika.

Von Reubens

3 cups shredded red cabbage
1/4 cup cider vinegar
1/4 cup packed brown sugar
8 rye bread slices

Roast beef slices
4 Kraft natural muenster
  cheese slices
Soft Parkay margarine

Combine cabbage, vinegar and sugar; mix lightly. Cook over low
heat 20 minutes; drain. For each sandwich, cover slice of bread with
meat, cabbage mixture and cheese; top with second slice of bread.
Spread bread with margarine; grill or broil on both sides until lightly
browned.   4 sandwiches

Chef Salad Sandwiches

3 cups torn lettuce
3/4 cup chopped tomato
2 hard-cooked eggs, chopped
1/4 cup Kraft French dressing
Kraft natural Swiss cheese slices

Kraft natural sharp cheddar
  cheese slices
6 individual French bread
  loaves, baked
Salami slices, quartered

Toss lettuce, tomato and eggs with dressing. Cut cheese into triangles. For each sandwich, cut top from bread loaf; remove center from bottom half of bread. Fill with salad mixture. Top with meat, Swiss and cheddar cheese and top half of bread.
6 sandwiches

Nice to know: Bread removed from center of loaf can be used to make fresh bread crumbs.

Reubenini

2 cups shredded cabbage
2 tablespoons Miracle Whip
  salad dressing
8 Italian bread slices
Salami slices

4 Kraft natural low moisture
  part-skim mozzarella cheese
  slices
Soft Parkay margarine

Combine cabbage and salad dressing; mix lightly. For each sandwich, cover slice of bread with salami, cabbage mixture and cheese; top with second slice of bread. Spread bread with margarine; grill or broil on both sides until lightly browned.   4 sandwiches

---

When sandwiches are to be transported or stored, keep vegetables like lettuce and tomatoes separate. Add them to the sandwiches just before eating.

Salami Reuben Sandwich

Rye bread slices
Kraft thousand island dressing
Kraft natural Swiss cheese slices

Salami slices
Sauerkraut, drained
Soft Parkay margarine

For each sandwich, spread two slices of bread with dressing. Cover one slice of bread with cheese, meat, sauerkraut and second slice of bread. Spread bread with margarine; grill on both sides until lightly browned.

Dilly Delights

1/2 cup dairy sour cream
2 teaspoons chopped dill pickle
4 onion rolls, split
Lettuce

Kraft muenster Singles
  pasteurized process cheese food
Luncheon meat slices

Combine sour cream and dill pickle. For each sandwich, cover bottom half of roll with lettuce, process cheese food and meat. Top with sour cream mixture; serve with top half of roll.   4 sandwiches

Big Boy Hero

Individual French bread loaves,
  baked, split
Miracle Whip salad dressing
Pickle relish
Assorted luncheon meats

Deluxe Choice American
  pasteurized process cheese,
  cut in half diagonally
Onion slices
Tomato slices

For each sandwich, spread half of loaf with salad dressing. Top with pickle relish, meat, cheese, onion and tomato. Serve with top half of loaf.

Kids Special Grill

White bread slices
Miracle Whip salad dressing
Canned luncheon meat slices
Pickle relish

Velveeta pasteurized process
  cheese spread, sliced
Soft Parkay margarine

For each sandwich, spread 2 slices of bread with salad dressing. Cover one slice of bread with meat, pickle relish and process cheese spread. Top with second slice of bread. Spread bread with margarine; grill on both sides until lightly browned.

Beefy Supper Sandwiches

1/4 cup Parkay margarine
1/4 cup flour
2 cups milk
Dash of pepper
1 3-ounce package smoked
  sliced beef, chopped

2 tablespoons chopped pimiento
1 tablespoon chopped fresh
  parsley
8 white bread slices, toasted
Kraft American Singles
  pasteurized process cheese food

Make a white sauce with margarine, flour, milk and pepper. Stir in meat, pimiento and parsley; heat. For each sandwich, cover slice of toast with process cheese food; broil until melted. Top with sauce.   8 sandwiches

Royal Chicken Sandwiches

4 Italian bread slices, toasted
Cooked chicken or turkey slices

Kraft monterey jack Singles
   pasteurized process cheese food
Palatial Sauce

For each sandwich, cover slice of toast with chicken and process cheese food. Top with:

Palatial Sauce

1/2 cup Kraft real mayonnaise
1/4 cup chili sauce
2 tablespoons finely chopped
   celery

2 tablespoons finely chopped
   green pepper
1 tablespoon chopped pimiento

Combine ingredients; mix well.   1 cup sauce for 4 sandwiches

Variation: Substitute Kraft Swiss Singles pasteurized process cheese food for monterey jack Singles.

Chicken 'n Nut Lunch

2 cups chopped cooked chicken
1/2 cup chopped peanuts
1 tablespoon chopped chives
1/4 teaspoon salt
Miracle Whip salad dressing

16 white bread slices
Soft Parkay margarine
Kraft American Singles
   pasteurized process cheese food

Combine chicken, nuts, chives, salt and enough salad dressing to moisten; mix lightly. Spread bread with margarine. For each sandwich, cover slice of bread with process cheese food and chicken mixture. Top with second slice of process cheese food and bread.   8 sandwiches

Nice to know: These sandwiches can be frozen. Wrap in aluminum foil or plastic wrap; freeze. Thaw 2 to 4 hours.

Turkey Tempter

Whole wheat bread slices
Kraft real mayonnaise
Lettuce

Deluxe Choice sharp • Old English
   pasteurized process cheese
Cooked turkey slices
Whole berry cranberry sauce

For each sandwich, spread slice of bread with mayonnaise. Cover with lettuce, cheese and turkey. Repeat layers; top with cranberry sauce.

Bacon and Tomato Grill

White bread slices   Tomato slices
Kraft American Singles   Crisply cooked bacon slices
  pasteurized process cheese food   Miracle Whip salad dressing

For each sandwich, cover slice of bread with process cheese food, tomato, bacon and second slice of process cheese food. Spread bread with salad dressing; grill on both sides until lightly browned.

Brunch Special

White bread slices   Tomato slices
Cheez Whiz pasteurized process   Crisply cooked bacon slices
  cheese spread   Miracle Whip salad dressing
Lettuce

For each sandwich, spread one slice of bread with process cheese spread. Top with lettuce, tomato, bacon and second slice of bread, spread with salad dressing.

Swiss Bacon Grill

Rye bread slices   Crisply cooked bacon slices
Kraft Swiss Singles   Soft Parkay margarine
  pasteurized process cheese food

For each sandwich, cover slice of bread with process cheese food and bacon. Top with second slice of process cheese food and bread. Spread bread with margarine; grill on both sides until lightly browned.

Make sandwiches more interesting and attractive with appropriate garnishes like fruit, vegetables, relish or pickles.

Sicilian Sandwich

Italian bread slices, toasted   Green pepper rings
Parkay margarine   Kraft natural provolone
Crisply cooked bacon slices   cheese slices
Tomato slices   Sweet cherry peppers

For each sandwich, spread slice of toast with margarine. Top with bacon, tomato, green pepper and cheese. Broil until cheese melts. Garnish with pepper.

Toasty Tuna Sandwiches

1 6 1/2-ounce can tuna, drained,
   flaked
1/4 pound Velveeta pasteurized
   process cheese spread, cubed
1/4 cup chopped celery
1 hard-cooked egg, chopped

1 tablespoon chopped onion
Dash of pepper
Kraft real mayonnaise
6 white bread slices, toasted
Tomato slices

Combine tuna, process cheese spread, celery, egg, onion, pepper and enough mayonnaise to moisten; mix lightly. For each sandwich, cover slice of toast with tuna mixture; top with tomato. Place on ungreased cookie sheet. Bake at 350°, 10 minutes.
6 sandwiches

Tuna Salad Hawaiian

1 6 1/2-ounce can tuna, drained,
   flaked
1/2 cup celery slices
1/2 cup chopped apple
1 8 1/4-ounce can crushed
   pineapple, drained

Miracle Whip salad dressing
12 white bread slices
Kraft American Singles
   pasteurized process cheese food

Combine tuna, celery, fruit and enough salad dressing to moisten; mix lightly. For each sandwich, cover slice of bread with process cheese food, tuna mixture and additional process cheese food. Top with second slice of bread.   6 sandwiches

Tuna Take Alongs

1 6 1/2-ounce can tuna, drained,
   flaked
2 tablespoons finely chopped
   celery
2 tablespoons Kraft real
   mayonnaise

1 tablespoon finely chopped
   onion
4 hamburger buns, split
Kraft American Singles
   pasteurized process cheese food
Tomato slices

Combine tuna, celery, mayonnaise and onion; mix lightly. For each sandwich, cover bottom half of bun with process cheese food, tuna mixture, tomato slice, process cheese food and top half of bun. Wrap each sandwich in heavy aluminum foil. Place sandwich, top side down, on grill; grill over low coals 10 minutes. Turn; grill 10 minutes longer.   4 sandwiches

Variation: Bake wrapped sandwiches at 425°, 15 minutes

Blue Cheese Burgers

1 pound ground beef
1 cup (4 ounces) crumbled
  Casino brand natural blue
  cheese

4 hamburger buns, split
Soft Parkay margarine

Shape meat into 8 thin patties. For each sandwich, place 2 table-spoons cheese on a patty. Top with second patty; seal edges. Broil on both sides to desired doneness. Spread bottom half of bun with margarine; top with patty and additional 2 tablespoons of cheese. Serve with top half of bun.   4 sandwiches

Cantonese Burgers

1 pound ground beef
1 16-ounce can bean sprouts,
  drained
Soy sauce
1/2 teaspoon onion salt

Kraft American Singles
  pasteurized process cheese food
6 sesame seed buns, split
6 pineapple rings
Miracle Whip salad dressing

Combine meat, bean sprouts, 2 tablespoons soy sauce and onion salt. Shape into six patties. Broil or grill on both sides to desired doneness. Top with process cheese food; heat until process cheese food melts. For each sandwich, cover bottom half of bun with patty and grilled pineapple ring, brushed with soy sauce. Serve with top half of bun spread with salad dressing.   6 sandwiches

Spudburgers

1 pound ground beef
1 cup shredded potato
1/4 cup chopped onion
1 teaspoon salt
Dash of pepper

Kraft American Singles
  pasteurized process cheese food
5 Kaiser rolls, split, toasted
5 red onion slices
Mushroom slices

Combine meat, potato, onion and seasonings. Shape into 5 patties. Broil or grill on both sides to desired doneness. Top with process cheese food; heat until process cheese food melts. For each sand-wich, cover bottom half of bun with patty, onion slice and mush-rooms. Serve with top half of bun.   5 sandwiches

Opposite: Blue Cheese Burgers, Cantonese Burgers, Spudburgers

Seaburgers

2 6 1/2-ounce cans tuna,   Dash of salt and pepper
   drained, flaked   Parkay margarine
2/3 cup Kraft real mayonnaise   6 hamburger buns, split, toasted
1/2 cup chopped celery   Kraft brick Singles
Dry bread crumbs   pasteurized process cheese food
2 tablespoons chopped onion
2 tablespoons chopped fresh
   parsley

Combine tuna, mayonnaise, celery, 1/4 cup bread crumbs, onion, parsley and seasonings; mix lightly. Shape into eight patties; coat with bread crumbs. Cook on both sides in small amount of margarine until browned. For each sandwich, cover bottom half of bun with patty and process cheese food; broil until process cheese food melts. Serve with top half of bun.   8 sandwiches

Golden Fruit Grills

1 8 1/4-ounce can crushed   12 white bread slices
   pineapple, well drained   Velveeta pasteurized process
1/2 cup chopped apple   cheese spread, sliced
1/4 cup raisins   Soft Parkay margarine
Miracle Whip salad dressing

Combine pineapple, apple, raisins and enough salad dressing to moisten; mix lightly. For each sandwich, cover slice of bread with process cheese spread. Top with fruit mixture and second slice of bread. Spread bread with margarine; grill on both sides until lightly browned.   6 sandwiches

Shrimpjohn Sandwiches

1 8-ounce package Philadelphia   Dash of salt and pepper
   Brand cream cheese   4 individual French bread
1 tablespoon milk   loaves, baked, split
2 teaspoons lemon juice   1 4 1/2-ounce can shrimp,
1 tablespoon green onion slices   drained, rinsed
1/2 teaspoon Worcestershire sauce Chopped fresh parsley

Combine softened cream cheese, milk and lemon juice, mixing until well blended. Add onion, Worcestershire sauce and seasonings; mix well. For each sandwich, spread both halves of loaf with cream cheese mixture. Top with shrimp; sprinkle with parsley.
4 sandwiches

Hoagy's Hot Dog Sandwich

*Individual French bread
   loaves, baked, split
Shredded lettuce
Dill pickle slices
Frankfurters, heated, split*

*Kraft sharp natural cheddar
   cheese, shredded
Chili sauce
Chopped onion*

For each sandwich, cover bottom half of loaf with lettuce, pickles, frankfurter, cheese, chili sauce and onion. Serve with top half of loaf.

Garden Patch Sandwiches

*1/2 cup soft Parkay margarine
1 tablespoon minced zucchini
1 tablespoon minced carrot
1 tablespoon minced celery
1 tablespoon minced green
   pepper*

*White bread slices
Kraft natural Swiss cheese
   slices, cut in half*

Combine margarine, zucchini, carrot, celery and green pepper. For each sandwich, spread two slices of bread with margarine mixture. Cover one slice of bread with cheese and second slice of bread. 4 to 5 sandwiches

Coastal Special

*Frankfurter buns, split
Tartar sauce
4-inch frozen fish sticks,
   cooked*

*Deluxe Choice American
   pasteurized process cheese,
   cut in half*

For each sandwich, spread bottom half of bun with tartar sauce. Top with fish, cheese and top half of bun.

Hawaiian Grill

*White bread slices
Deluxe Choice American
   pasteurized process cheese*

*Pineapple slices
Soft Parkay margarine*

For each sandwich, cover slice of bread with cheese, pineapple and additional cheese. Top with second slice of bread. Spread bread with margarine; grill on both sides until lightly browned.

Chapter 10
Sauce Sorcery

Savory Cheese Sauce

1/3 cup chopped celery
1/3 cup chopped onion
2 tablespoons Parkay margarine
2 tablespoons flour
1/2 teaspoon salt

Dash of pepper
1 cup milk
1 1/2 cups (6 ounces) shredded
    Casino brand natural monterey
    jack cheese

Sauté celery and onion in margarine; blend in flour and seasonings. Gradually add milk; cook, stirring constantly, until thickened. Add cheese; continue cooking until cheese is melted. Serve over hot vegetables.   2 cups

Apple Country Rabbit

2 cups (8 ounces) shredded Kraft
    sharp natural cheddar cheese
1/2 cup apple juice
2 tablespoons Parkay margarine
1 egg, slightly beaten

White bread slices, toasted,
    cut in half diagonally or
    English muffins, split, toasted
Pork sausage links, cooked

Heat cheese, apple juice and margarine in double boiler or in saucepan over low heat; stir until smooth. Add egg; stir until thickened. Serve over toast or English muffins; top with sausage.   4 servings

---

Cheez Whiz pasteurized process cheese spread makes a quick, flavorful sauce. Just heat it and serve over vegetables, macaroni or even over Canadian bacon and poached eggs for a simplified Eggs Benedict.

Mornay Sauce

1/4 cup Parkay margarine
1/4 cup flour
1/2 teaspoon salt
Dash of pepper
2 cups milk

1 cup (4 ounces) shredded Kraft
    natural Swiss cheese
1/4 cup (1 ounce) Kraft grated
    parmesan cheese

Melt margarine in saucepan over low heat. Blend in flour and seasonings. Gradually add milk; cook, stirring constantly, until thickened. Add cheeses; stir until melted. Serve over hot cooked broccoli, asparagus, sliced turkey or ham.   2 3/4 cups

Nice to know: This sauce can be refrigerated and then reheated.

Opposite: Savory Cheese Sauce, Apple Country Rabbit

Regal Cheese Sauce

1 8-ounce package Philadelphia
  Brand cream cheese, cubed
1/2 cup milk

1/4 teaspoon garlic salt
1/4 cup (1 ounce) Kraft grated
  parmesan cheese

Heat cream cheese and milk over low heat; stir until sauce is smooth. Blend in remaining ingredients. Serve over hot vegetables. 1 3/4 cups

Jubilee Sauce

1 8-ounce package Philadelphia
  Brand cream cheese
1/2 cup dairy sour cream
1/4 cup sugar

1/4 cup Kraft pure 100%
  pasteurized orange juice
Assorted fruit

Combine softened cream cheese, sour cream and sugar, mixing until well blended. Stir in orange juice; chill. Serve over fruit. 2 cups

---

A tasty, quick rabbit can be made by heating Cheez Whiz pasteurized process cheese spread and serving it over thick toast, topped with cooked bacon, slices of tomato, or both.

Continental Sauce

2 tablespoons Parkay margarine
2 tablespoons flour
1/2 teaspoon salt

1 1/4 cups milk
1/4 cup (1 ounce) Kraft grated
  parmesan cheese

Melt margarine in saucepan over low heat. Blend in flour and salt. Gradually add milk; cook, stirring constantly, until thickened. Add cheese; stir until well blended. Serve over hot green vegetables. 1 1/3 cups

Variation: Add dash of Tabasco sauce.

Cheddar Cheese Sauce

2 tablespoons Parkay margarine
2 tablespoons flour
1/4 teaspoon salt
Dash of cayenne

Dash of dry mustard
1 cup milk
1 cup (4 ounces) shredded Kraft
  sharp natural cheddar cheese

Melt margarine in saucepan over low heat. Blend in flour and seasonings. Gradually add milk; cook, stirring constantly, until thickened. Add cheese; stir until melted. 1 1/3 cups

Golden Sauce

1/2 pound Velveeta pasteurized   1/4 cup milk
  process cheese spread, cubed

Heat process cheese spread and milk over low heat; stir until sauce is smooth.   1 cup

Variations: Add a 2 1/2-ounce jar chopped, drained mushrooms.
            Add 4 crisply cooked bacon slices, crumbled.
            Add 1 tablespoon of chopped pimiento.

Savory Golden Sauce

2 tablespoons finely chopped   1 tablespoon Parkay margarine
  celery   1/2 pound Velveeta pasteurized
2 tablespoons finely chopped   process cheese spread, cubed
  onion   1/4 cup milk

Sauté celery and onion in margarine. Add process cheese spread and milk; heat until sauce is smooth. Serve over hot cauliflower or broccoli.   1 cup

Variation: Substitute finely chopped green pepper for celery; serve over hot cauliflower.

When making a cheese sauce from natural cheese, shred the cheese for easy melting. When using process cheese, cube or slice the cheese instead.

California Crab Rabbit

1/2 cup chopped celery   1 1/2 cups (7 1/2-ounce can)
1/4 cup chopped onion   drained, flaked crabmeat
2 tablespoons Parkay margarine   2 tablespoons chopped fresh
2 tablespoons flour   parsley
1 1/2 cups milk   1 tablespoon lemon juice
2 cups (8 ounces) shredded   White bread slices, toasted,
  Casino brand natural monterey   cut in half diagonally
  jack cheese

Sauté celery and onion in margarine; blend in flour. Add milk; cook, stirring constantly, until thickened. Add cheese; continue cooking until cheese is melted. Add crabmeat, parsley and lemon juice; heat. Serve over toast.   6 servings

"Philly" Chocolate Sauce

1 8-ounce package Philadelphia
  Brand cream cheese, cubed
1/3 cup milk
2 1-ounce squares unsweetened
  chocolate

2 cups confectioners' sugar
1 teaspoon vanilla

Heat cream cheese, milk and chocolate over low heat; stir until sauce is smooth. Blend in remaining ingredients. Serve warm over ice cream, pound cake or fruit.   2 cups

Nice to know: This sauce can be refrigerated and then reheated.

Serve a satisfying and hearty rabbit by topping it with slices of cooked ham or small chunks of cooked chicken. It's ideal for a quick lunch or a light supper.

"Philly" Sauce Supreme
with Savoy Sandwiches

1/2 cup milk
1 8-ounce package Philadelphia
  Brand cream cheese, cubed
1/4 cup (1 ounce) Kraft grated
  parmesan cheese

1/2 teaspoon onion salt
Savoy Sandwiches

Heat milk and cream cheese over low heat, stirring until smooth. Blend in parmesan cheese and onion salt. Serve over Savoy Sandwiches.   1/2 cup

Savoy Sandwiches

2 tablespoons chopped green
  pepper
2 tablespoons Parkay margarine
4 eggs, beaten
1/4 teaspoon salt

Dash of pepper
3 English muffins, split, toasted
6 Canadian-style bacon slices,
  cooked
"Philly" Sauce Supreme

Sauté green pepper in margarine. Combine eggs and seasonings; pour into skillet. Cook slowly, stirring occasionally, until eggs are cooked. For each sandwich, cover muffin half with bacon and scrambled eggs. Top with "Philly" Sauce Supreme.   6 sandwiches

Opposite: "Philly" Chocolate Sauce

Chive Sauce with
Turkey in the Rye

1/2 cup Miracle Whip salad   2 teaspoons chopped chives
   dressing   Turkey in the Rye

Combine salad dressing and chives; mix well. Serve over Turkey in the Rye.   1/2 cup

Turkey in the Rye

4 rye bread slices   Turkey slices
Kraft American Singles   Cucumber slices
   pasteurized process cheese food   Chive Sauce

For each sandwich, cover slice of bread with process cheese food, turkey and cucumber. Top with Chive Sauce.   4 sandwiches

Dill Sauce with Maritime Dinner

1 8-ounce package Philadelphia   1/2 teaspoon dill weed
   Brand cream cheese, cubed   1/4 teaspoon salt
1/2 cup milk   Maritime Dinner

Heat cream cheese and milk over low heat; stir until sauce is smooth. Blend in remaining ingredients. Serve over Maritime Dinner.   2 cups

Maritime Dinner

2 eggs, slightly beaten   Dash of pepper
1/4 cup milk   1 pound fish fillets
1 tablespoon lemon juice   1 1/4 cups dry bread crumbs
1/2 teaspoon salt   All purpose oil

Combine eggs, milk, lemon juice and seasonings; mix well. Dip fish in egg mixture; coat with bread crumbs. Repeat. Fry on both sides in small amount of oil until fish is browned and flakes easily with a fork. Serve with Dill Sauce.   4 servings

Quick Rabbit Supper

1 8-ounce jar Cheez Whiz   8 tomato slices
   pasteurized process cheese   4 white bread slices, toasted
   spread   8 crisply cooked bacon slices

Heat process cheese spread in saucepan over low heat. For each serving, place 2 tomato slices on slice of toast. Top with process cheese spread and bacon.   4 servings

Redwood Rabbit

1/4 cup Parkay margarine
1/4 cup flour
1 1/2 cups milk
1/2 cup beer
2 cups (8 ounces) shredded
  Casino brand natural brick
  cheese

White bread slices, toasted,
  cut in half diagonally
4 crisply cooked bacon slices,
  crumbled

Melt margarine in saucepan over low heat. Blend in flour. Gradually add milk; cook, stirring constantly, until thickened. Stir in beer. Add cheese; continue cooking until cheese is melted. Serve over toast; sprinkle with bacon. 4 servings

Welsh Rabbit

1/4 cup Parkay margarine
1/4 cup flour
1/2 teaspoon salt
Dash of pepper
Dash of dry mustard
2 cups milk

1/2 pound Old English sharp
  pasteurized process American
  cheese, cubed
White bread slices, toasted,
  cut in half diagonally

Melt margarine in saucepan over low heat. Blend in flour and seasonings. Gradually add milk; cook, stirring constantly, until thickened. Add cheese; stir until melted. Serve over toast triangles. Garnish with paprika, if desired. 4 to 6 servings

Cheddar cheese sauce adds flavor and color to vegetables, and it's easy to make!

Classic Cheese Rabbit

2 cups (8 ounces) shredded
  Cracker Barrel brand sharp
  natural cheddar cheese
1/2 cup beer or ale
2 tablespoons Parkay margarine

1/2 teaspoon paprika
1/4 teaspoon dry mustard
1 egg, slightly beaten
White bread slices, toasted,
  cut in half diagonally

Heat cheese, beer, margarine and seasonings in double boiler or saucepan over low heat; stir until smooth. Blend in egg; stir until thickened. Serve over toast. 4 servings

Variations: Stir in 6 crisply cooked bacon slices, crumbled.
            Top with French fried onions.
            Top with hard-cooked egg slices.
            Serve over shoestring potatoes.

Chapter 11
Eye Openers —
Breakfast and Brunch

Saucy Breakfast Sandwiches

1/4 cup Parkay margarine
1/4 cup flour
2 cups milk
Dash of pepper
1 3-ounce package smoked sliced
  beef, chopped

2 hard-cooked eggs, chopped
8 white bread slices, toasted
Kraft American Singles
  pasteurized process cheese food

Make a white sauce with margarine, flour, milk and pepper; stir in meat and eggs. Heat. For each sandwich, cover slice of toast with process cheese food; broil until melted. Top with sauce.
8 sandwiches

Spoon fresh fruit on a wedge of honeydew melon, then top it with Philadelphia Brand Whipped cream cheese for a special breakfast treat.

Savory Scrambled Eggs

2 tablespoons Parkay margarine
6 eggs, beaten
1/3 cup milk

Salt and pepper
1 3-ounce package Philadelphia
  Brand cream cheese, cubed

Melt margarine in skillet over low heat; add combined eggs, milk and seasonings. Cook slowly, stirring until eggs begin to thicken. Add cream cheese; continue cooking, stirring occasionally, until cream cheese is melted and eggs are cooked.   4 servings

Variations: Add chopped fresh parsley, chives, green onion slices or crisply cooked crumbled bacon as eggs begin to thicken.
Substitute any of the following for cream cheese:
  1 cup (4 ounces) shredded Kraft sharp natural cheddar cheese.
  1/2 cup (2 ounces) shredded Kraft natural Swiss cheese.
  1/4 pound Velveeta pasteurized process cheese spread, cubed.
  1/2 cup Cheez Whiz pasteurized process cheese spread.

Opposite: Saucy Breakfast Sandwiches, Savory Scrambled Eggs

Hacienda Brunch

1/2 cup chopped celery
1/4 cup green onion slices
1 tablespoon Parkay margarine
1 cup Kraft barbecue sauce

*   *   *

1/4 cup Parkay margarine
8 eggs, beaten

1/4 cup milk
1 8-ounce jar Cheez Whiz
  pasteurized process cheese
  spread
3 English muffins, split, toasted
  or 6 corn tortillas, crisply fried

Sauté celery and onion in margarine. Add barbecue sauce; simmer 15 minutes.

Melt margarine in skillet over low heat; add combined eggs and milk. Cook slowly, stirring occasionally, until eggs begin to thicken. Add 1/2 cup process cheese spread; continue cooking, stirring occasionally, until process cheese spread is melted and eggs are cooked. Spread muffin halves with remaining process cheese spread. For each serving, cover muffin half with eggs; top with sauce.
6 servings

Sunday Brunch

1/4 pound bulk sausage
1/2 cup chopped onion
8 eggs, beaten
1/2 cup milk

1/4 teaspoon salt
Dash of pepper
1 8-ounce package Philadelphia
  Brand cream cheese, cubed

Brown sausage and onion; drain. Add combined eggs, milk and seasonings. Cook slowly, stirring until eggs begin to thicken. Add cream cheese; continue cooking, stirring occasionally, until cheese is melted and eggs are cooked.   6 servings

> To make poached eggs on toast a special treat, heat Cheez Whiz pasteurized process cheese spread and spoon it over the eggs.

Dynasty Eggs

2 tablespoons Parkay margarine
2 tablespoons flour
1 1/2 cups milk
1/2 teaspoon salt
4 hard-cooked eggs, quartered

1 6-ounce can water chestnuts,
  drained, sliced
2 tablespoons green onion slices
4 English muffins, split, toasted
Deluxe Choice American
  pasteurized process cheese

Make a white sauce with margarine, flour, milk and salt. Add eggs, water chestnuts and onion; heat. For each serving, cover muffin half with cheese; broil until cheese begins to melt. Top with egg mixture.   8 servings

Georgian Creamed Eggs

1/4 cup Parkay margarine
1/4 cup flour
2 cups milk
1/2 teaspoon salt
Dash of cayenne

6 hard-cooked eggs, sliced
2 tablespoons chopped pimiento
1 tablespoon chopped chives
Golden Cheddar Corn Bread

Make a white sauce with margarine, flour, milk and seasonings. Stir in eggs, pimiento and chives; heat. Serve over:

Golden Cheddar Corn Bread

1 cup cornmeal
1 cup flour
1 tablespoon baking powder
1 1/2 teaspoons salt

2 cups (8 ounces) shredded Kraft
   sharp natural cheddar cheese
1 cup milk
1/4 cup Parkay margarine, melted
1 egg, beaten

Combine dry ingredients; stir in cheese. Combine milk, margarine and egg; add to dry ingredients, mixing until just moistened. Pour into greased 8-inch square baking pan. Bake at 425°, 35 minutes.   6 servings

Saucy Chicken

1/2 cup celery slices
1/4 cup chopped onion
1/4 cup chopped green pepper
1/4 cup Parkay margarine
3 tablespoons flour
3/4 cup milk
1 8-ounce jar Cheez Whiz
   pasteurized process cheese
   spread or Cheez Whiz
   with pimento

1 2 1/2-ounce jar mushrooms,
   drained
1/3 cup slivered almonds, toasted
2 cups chopped cooked chicken
Toast or biscuits

Sauté celery, onion and green pepper in margarine. Blend in flour. Gradually add milk; cook, stirring constantly, until thickened. Add process cheese spread; stir until melted. Add remaining ingredients; heat, stirring constantly. Serve over toast.   6 servings

Alpine Oven Omelet

6 eggs, separated
2 tablespoons milk
1/2 teaspoon salt
2 tablespoons chopped chives

1 8-ounce package Kraft natural
    Swiss cheese slices, cut into
    thin strips
1 2 1/2-ounce jar sliced
    mushrooms, drained

Combine egg yolks, milk and salt; beat until thick and lemon colored. Add chives and two-thirds of cheese. Fold into stiffly beaten egg whites. Pour into hot, well greased 10-inch ovenproof skillet. Cook over low heat 10 minutes or until underside is golden brown. Bake at 325°, 10 to 15 minutes or until top is firm. Remove from oven; make a deep crease across center of top. Place mushrooms and remaining cheese on half of omelet. Slip spatula underneath, tip skillet to loosen and gently fold omelet in half.
6 to 8 servings

Puffy Omelet

1 8-ounce jar Cheez Whiz
    pasteurized process cheese
    spread

1/4 cup milk
6 eggs, separated
1/4 teaspoon cream of tartar

Heat process cheese spread and milk over low heat. Remove from heat; beat in egg yolks one at a time, mixing well after each addition. Beat egg whites until foamy; add cream of tartar, beating until stiff peaks form. Fold egg whites into cheese spread mixture. Pour into 10-inch ovenproof skillet. Bake at 325°, 45 to 50 minutes or until lightly browned.   6 servings

Variation: Bake in 12-inch ovenproof skillet, 30 to 35 minutes or until lightly browned.

Homesteader's Breakfast

6 bacon slices
4 cups chopped cooked potatoes
1/4 cup chopped green pepper
1/4 cup chopped onion

Salt and pepper
1 4-ounce package Kraft shredded
    sharp natural cheddar cheese

Fry bacon until crisp; remove from skillet. Drain fat, reserving 1/4 cup. Crumble bacon. Cook potato, green pepper and onion in reserved fat until lightly browned. Stir in bacon; top with cheese.
4 to 6 servings

Opposite: Alpine Oven Omelet

California Sunrise

1 8-ounce jar Cheez Whiz
    pasteurized process cheese
    spread
1/4 cup chopped green pepper

1 tablespoon Parkay margarine
6 eggs, beaten
1/4 cup chopped pimiento
Avocado slices

Heat process cheese spread over low heat. In a 10-inch skillet, saute green pepper in margarine. Combine process cheese spread with eggs and pimiento. Pour egg mixture into skillet; stir. Cover; cook over low heat 30 to 35 minutes or until egg mixture is set. Garnish with avocado slices.   4 servings

---

Make brunch a special event by serving hot pancakes with dollops of whipped cream cheese topped with strawberry preserves.

Heritage Omelet

2 tablespoons Parkay margarine
6 eggs, slightly beaten
1/3 cup milk
Salt and pepper
1 2 1/2-ounce jar mushrooms,
    drained

1 teaspoon finely chopped chives
1 cup (4 ounces) shredded Kraft
    sharp natural cheddar cheese

Melt margarine in 10-inch skillet over low heat. Combine eggs, milk and seasonings; pour into skillet. Cook slowly. As egg mixture sets, lift slightly with a spatula to allow uncooked portion to flow underneath. When set, cover omelet with mushrooms, chives and 3/4 cup cheese. Fold in half; sprinkle with remaining cheese. 3 to 4 servings

Southern-Style Creamed Chicken

1/2 cup chopped onion
3 tablespoons Parkay margarine
2 tablespoons flour
1/2 teaspoon salt
Dash of cayenne
1 1/2 cups milk
1 1/2 cups (6 ounces) shredded
    Kraft sharp natural cheddar
    cheese

1/4 cup Kraft real mayonnaise
1 1/2 cups chopped cooked chicken
1 10-ounce package frozen peas,
    cooked, drained
4 hard-cooked eggs, sliced
1 4-ounce can mushrooms, drained
6 corn bread squares

Saute onion in margarine. Blend in flour and seasonings. Gradually add milk; cook, stirring constantly, until thickened. Add cheese; stir until melted. Blend in mayonnaise. Add chicken, peas, eggs and mushrooms; heat thoroughly. Serve over corn bread.   6 servings

Apples 'n Sausage Heidelberg

1 pound pork sausage links
12 apple rings
2 tablespoons brown sugar
1/4 teaspoon cinnamon

1 cup (4 ounces) shredded
   Casino brand natural muenster
   cheese

Brown meat; remove from skillet. Drain fat, reserving 1/4 cup. Sauté apple rings in reserved fat. Place rings on rack of broiler pan. Sprinkle with combined sugar and cinnamon; top with sausage links and cheese. Broil until cheese melts.   6 to 8 servings

Swiss Omelet Special

4 eggs, beaten
2 tablespoons milk
2 tablespoons chopped pimiento
1/2 teaspoon onion salt
Dash of pepper

Parkay margarine
Chopped green pepper
4 Vienna bread slices, toasted
Kraft natural Swiss cheese slices

Combine eggs, milk, pimiento and seasonings. Make individual omelets. For each omelet, melt 2 teaspoons margarine in 6-inch skillet or omelet pan over low heat. Sauté 2 teaspoons green pepper. Pour 1/3 cup egg mixture into skillet. Cook slowly. As egg mixture sets, lift slightly with a spatula to allow uncooked portion to flow underneath. When set, fold in half. For each sandwich, cover slice of bread with cheese; broil until cheese melts. Top with omelet.   4 sandwiches

---

For a special breakfast treat, spread toasted English muffins with whipped cream cheese, top with slices of fruit and drizzle with honey.

Sausage 'n Egg Brunch

1 tablespoon Parkay margarine
4 eggs, beaten
2 tablespoons milk
Salt and pepper
4 white bread slices, toasted

Kraft natural low moisture
   part-skim mozzarella cheese
   slices, cut in half
4 pork sausage links, cooked,
   split lengthwise

Melt margarine in skillet over low heat; add combined eggs, milk and seasonings. Cook slowly, stirring occasionally, until eggs are cooked. For each sandwich, cover slice of bread with cheese. Broil until cheese begins to melt. Top with hot sausage and eggs.
4 sandwiches

Apple Dandy

6 raisin bread slices, toasted
Soft Parkay margarine
12 crisply cooked bacon slices
Thin apple slices

Brown sugar
Velveeta pasteurized process
  cheese spread, sliced

For each sandwich, spread toast with margarine; top with 2 bacon slices and apple slices. Sprinkle lightly with brown sugar. Broil until sugar bubbles. Cover with process cheese spread; continue broiling until process cheese spread melts.   6 sandwiches

Canadian Bacon and Egg Sandwiches

2 tablespoons Parkay margarine
6 eggs, slightly beaten
1/3 cup milk
Salt and pepper
3 English muffins, split, toasted

6 hot cooked Canadian-style
  bacon slices
Velveeta pasteurized process
  cheese spread, sliced

Melt margarine in skillet over low heat; add combined eggs, milk and seasonings. Cook slowly, stirring occasionally until eggs are cooked. For each sandwich, cover muffin half with bacon slice, scrambled eggs and process cheese spread. Broil until process cheese spread melts.   6 sandwiches

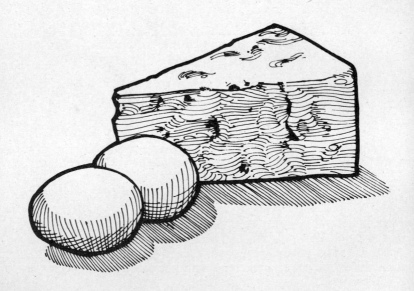

Waffled Breakfast Sandwich

White bread slices
Thin apple slices
Crisply cooked bacon slices

Kraft American Singles
   pasteurized process cheese food
Soft Parkay margarine

For each sandwich, cover slice of bread with apples, bacon and process cheese food; top with second slice of bread. Spread bread with margarine; grill in hot waffle iron until lightly browned.

Belgian Waffles Elegante

1 cup Kraft marshmallow creme
1 8-ounce package Philadelphia
   Brand cream cheese
2 tablespoons orange juice

1 teaspoon grated orange rind
6 waffles
4 cups strawberry slices or
   halves

Combine marshmallow creme and softened cream cheese, mixing until well blended. Stir in orange juice and rind. For each serving, cover warm waffle with strawberries and cream cheese mixture. 6 servings

---

Serve your favorite creamed meat mixture for brunch (chicken, chipped beef or cooked ham) over crusty slices of French bread with lots of cheddar cheese melted on the bread.

"Philly" Creamed Eggs

1 tablespoon green onion slices
1 tablespoon Parkay margarine
1 8-ounce package Philadelphia
   Brand cream cheese, cubed
3/4 cup milk
3 hard-cooked eggs, sliced
1 teaspoon lemon juice

1/4 teaspoon salt
Dash of pepper
3 English muffins, split, toasted
Hot cooked pork sausage links,
   Canadian-style bacon or cooked
   ham slices

Sauté onion in margarine. Add cream cheese and milk. Cook over low heat; stir until sauce is smooth. Blend in eggs, lemon juice and seasonings. For each serving, cover muffin half with sausage; top with sauce.   6 servings

Sweet and Spicy Omelet

1 cup apple slices
3 tablespoons Parkay margarine
6 eggs, beaten
1/3 cup milk
1/2 teaspoon salt

Dash of pepper
1 cup (4 ounces) shredded Kraft
  sharp natural cheddar cheese
1 tablespoon brown sugar

Sauté apple slices in 1 tablespoon margarine in 10-inch skillet. Remove apples, add remaining margarine to skillet and melt over low heat. Combine eggs, milk and seasonings; pour into skillet. Cook slowly. As egg mixture sets, lift slightly with a spatula to allow uncooked portion to flow underneath. When set, cover omelet with 3/4 cup cheese, apples and sugar. Fold in half; sprinkle with remaining cheese.   3 to 4 servings

---

Add flavor and variety to breakfast by melting your favorite cheese (cheddar, Swiss or brick) on toast. Serve plain or topped with slices of crisp bacon.

Golden Jelly Strata

12 white bread slices
Kraft American Singles
  pasteurized process cheese food
4 eggs, beaten
2 cups milk

1 teaspoon salt
1/4 teaspoon dry mustard
Dash of pepper
Kraft concord grape jelly or
  strawberry preserves

Place four slices of bread in greased 9-inch square pan. Cover with four process cheese food slices and four slices of bread; repeat. Combine eggs, milk and seasoning; pour over bread. Cover; refrigerate 1 hour or overnight. Bake at 325°, 40 minutes or until lightly browned and puffy; let stand 5 minutes. Top with jelly; cut into squares.   4 to 6 servings

Breakfast Crunch

1 egg, slightly beaten
2 tablespoons milk
8 white bread slices
Kraft strawberry preserves

4 cooked ham slices
Kraft sharp Singles pasteurized
  process cheese food
3/4 cup crushed corn flakes

Combine egg and milk. For each sandwich, spread slice of bread with preserves. Cover with meat, process cheese food and second slice of bread. Dip sandwich in egg mixture, then in corn flakes, turning to coat both sides. Bake at 350°, 15 minutes.   4 sandwiches

"Philly" Orange Scones

1 8-ounce package Philadelphia Brand cream cheese	3 cups flour
1/2 cup sugar	1 tablespoon baking powder
1/3 cup nuts	1 1/2 teaspoons salt
2 tablespoons grated orange rind	1/2 cup Parkay margarine
* * *	1 cup milk
	Honey

1 8-ounce package Philadelphia
  Brand cream cheese
1/2 cup sugar
1/3 cup nuts
2 tablespoons grated orange rind
  *   *   *

3 cups flour
1 tablespoon baking powder
1 1/2 teaspoons salt
1/2 cup Parkay margarine
1 cup milk
Honey

Combine softened cream cheese and sugar, mixing until well blended. Stir in nuts and rind.

Combine dry ingredients; cut in margarine until mixture resembles coarse crumbs. Stir in milk, mixing until just moistened. Divide dough in half. Roll each half into 9 x 12-inch rectangle. Spread one rectangle of dough with cheese mixture. Top with remaining dough. Cut into twelve 3-inch squares; cut each square in half diagonally. Place scones on ungreased cookie sheet. Bake at 425°, 12 to 15 minutes or until lightly browned. Drizzle with honey. 2 dozen

---

Grilled cheese sandwiches make great breakfast fare. Serve plain, or tuck in thin slices of apple, crisp bacon or slices of cooked ham.

Swiss and Bacon Frittata

6 eggs
1/4 cup chopped green onion
1/2 teaspoon salt
Dash of pepper
2 tablespoons Parkay margarine

6 crisply cooked bacon slices,
  crumbled
1 cup (4 ounces) shredded Kraft
  natural Swiss cheese

Beat eggs until frothy. Add onion, salt and pepper; mix well. Heat margarine in 10-inch ovenproof skillet over medium heat. Pour in egg mixture; sprinkle with bacon. Cook eggs until set; do not stir. Remove from heat; sprinkle with cheese. Broil until cheese melts. Loosen omelet from sides of pan; slide onto plate, cheese side up.   4 servings

Opposite: Golden Jelly Strata (page 168), Vegetables Romano (page 168)

Chapter 12
Microwave Magic

Golden Jelly Strata

12 white bread slices
Kraft American Singles
    pasteurized process cheese food
4 eggs, beaten
2 cups milk

1 teaspoon salt
1/4 teaspoon dry mustard
Dash of pepper
Kraft concord grape jelly or
    strawberry preserves

Place four slices of bread in bottom of greased 8-inch square baking dish. Cover with four process cheese slices and four slices of bread; repeat. Combine eggs, milk and seasonings; pour over bread. Cover; refrigerate 1 hour or overnight. Micro-cook 20 minutes, turning half turn after every 5 minutes; let stand a few minutes. Top with jelly; cut into squares.   4 to 6 servings

Vegetables Romano

3 medium zucchini, sliced
1 cup onion rings
3 tablespoons Parkay margarine

1/2 teaspoon salt
1 cup chopped tomato
Kraft grated romano cheese

Combine zucchini, onion, margarine and salt. Cover and micro-cook 9 minutes, stirring once. Add tomato. Micro-cook, uncovered, 5 minutes. Sprinkle with cheese before serving.   4 to 6 servings

Spinach Treat

1 8-ounce package Philadephia
    Brand cream cheese, cubed
2 tablespoons Parkay margarine
3/4 teaspoon salt
1/4 teaspoon Tabasco sauce

2 tablespoons milk
2 10-ounce packages frozen
    chopped spinach, cooked,
    drained
1 hard-cooked egg, finely chopped

Combine cream cheese, margarine, salt, Tabasco sauce and milk. Micro-cook 1 minute; stir. Micro-cook an additional minute or until cheese is melted. Stir in hot spinach. Top with egg.   6 to 8 servings

Continental Sauce

2 tablespoons Parkay margarine
2 tablespoons flour
1/2 teaspoon salt
Dash of Tabasco sauce

1 1/4 cups milk
1/4 cup (1 ounce) Kraft grated
    parmesan cheese

Micro-cook margarine 30 seconds. Blend in flour, salt and Tabasco sauce. Gradually stir in milk. Micro-cook 2 1/2 minutes or until sauce boils and thickens, stirring occasionally. Add cheese; micro-cook 30 seconds. Serve over hot green vegetables.   1 1/3 cups

Cheddar Cheese Sauce

2 tablespoons Parkay margarine
2 tablespoons flour
1/4 teaspoon salt
Dash of cayenne
Dash of dry mustard

1 cup milk
1 cup (4 ounces) shredded
    Cracker Barrel brand sharp
    natural cheddar cheese

Micro-cook margarine 30 seconds. Blend in flour, salt, cayenne and mustard. Gradually stir in milk. Micro-cook 1 minute; stir well. Micro-cook 1 1/2 to 2 minutes or until sauce boils and thickens. Stir after each minute. Add cheese; micro-cook 1 minute. Stir well. 1 1/3 cups

Golden Sauce

1/2 pound Velveeta pasteurized
    process cheese spread, cubed

1/4 cup milk

Place ingredients in dish. Micro-cook 1 minute; stir. Micro-cook 30 seconds; stir. Micro-cook an additional 30 seconds; stir.   1 cup

Regal Cheese Sauce

1 8-ounce package Philadelphia
    Brand cream cheese, cubed
1/2 cup milk

1/4 teaspoon garlic salt
1/4 cup (1 ounce) Kraft grated
    parmesan cheese

Place cream cheese and milk in dish. Micro-cook 1 minute; stir. Add remaining ingredients. Micro-cook 1 minute or until cheese is melted; stir. Serve over hot vegetables.   1 3/4 cups

"Philly" Chocolate Sauce

1 8-ounce package Philadelphia
    Brand cream cheese, cubed
1/3 cup milk
2 1-ounce squares unsweetened
    chocolate

2 cups confectioners' sugar
1 teaspoon vanilla

Place cream cheese, milk and chocolate in dish. Micro-cook 1 1/2 minutes; stir. Micro-cook additional 1 minute. Stir until smooth. Blend in remaining ingredients. Serve over ice cream, cake or fruit.   2 cups

Nice to know: This sauce may be refrigerated and then reheated.

If your microwave oven has variable power, be sure to cook dishes that contain cheese on medium or low setting.

Cream Cheese Pie

2 8-ounce packages Philadelphia
   Brand cream cheese
3/4 cup sugar
2 teaspoons lemon juice

1/2 teaspoon vanilla
3 eggs
1 9-inch graham cracker crust

Combine softened cream cheese, sugar, lemon juice and vanilla, mixing at medium speed on electric mixer until well blended. Add eggs, one at a time, mixing well after each addition. Pour into crust. Micro-cook 6 1/2 minutes, turning one-quarter turn after each 30 seconds.   6 to 8 servings

Nob Hill Potato Bisque

2 cups mashed potatoes
2 cups milk
1 8-ounce jar Cheez Whiz
   pasteurized process cheese
   spread

2 tablespoons green onion
   slices
Dash of pepper

Combine ingredients. Micro-cook 10 minutes, stirring occasionally.   4 to 6 servings

Variation: Add 2 tablespoons of dry white wine.

Creamy "Philly" Soup

2 tablespoons Parkay margarine
1/3 cup chopped green pepper
1/4 cup chopped onion
1/2 teaspoon salt
Dash of pepper
1 cup milk

1 chicken bouillon cube
1 cup boiling water
1 8 3/4-ounce can cream style
   corn
1 8-ounce package Philadelphia
   Brand cream cheese, cubed

Combine margarine, green pepper, onion and seasonings; micro-cook 1 minute. Add milk, bouillon cube, water and corn. Micro-cook 5 minutes; stir. Add cream cheese; micro-cook 3 minutes or until cheese is melted; stir.   4 servings

Tuna Cheemato Soup

1 10 3/4-ounce can condensed
   tomato soup
1 1/4 cups water
1 6 1/2-ounce can tuna, drained,
   flaked

1 8-ounce jar Cheez Whiz
   pasteurized process cheese
   spread
Dash of pepper

Combine all ingredients; micro-cook 4 to 6 minutes or until thoroughly heated, stirring occasionally.   4 servings

Tangy Corn and Tomato Chowder

2 tablespoons Parkay margarine
2 tablespoons flour
1 cup tomato juice
1 16-ounce can tomatoes
1 12-ounce can whole kernel
   corn, drained

1/4 cup (1 ounce) Kraft grated
   parmesan cheese
1/2 teaspoon celery salt
1/4 teaspoon onion powder
Dash of Tabasco sauce

Micro-cook margarine 30 seconds. Blend in flour. Gradually stir in tomato juice. Micro-cook 1 1/2 minutes; stir. Micro-cook 1 minute; add remaining ingredients. Micro-cook 5 1/2 minutes, stirring occasionally. Sprinkle with additional cheese, if desired.   4 servings

Southwestern Sloppy Joes

1/2 pound ground beef
1/4 cup chopped onion
1/4 cup chopped green pepper
1 18-ounce jar baked beans
1/2 cup Kraft barbecue sauce

Corn bread, cut into 3-inch
   squares
Kraft mild natural colby cheese
   slices, cut into triangles

Combine meat, onion and green pepper. Micro-cook 4 minutes; drain. Add baked beans and barbecue sauce; mix well. Micro-cook 10 minutes; stir. Split corn bread; top with cheese. Broil until cheese melts; spoon meat mixture over bread.   6 to 8 servings

Party Sloppy Joes

1/2 pound ground beef
1/4 cup chopped onion
1/2 pound frankfurters, sliced
3/4 cup Kraft barbecue sauce

1/4 cup sweet pickle relish
8 hamburger buns, split
Velveeta pasteurized process
   cheese spread, sliced

Combine meat and onion. Micro-cook 4 minutes; drain. Stir in frankfurters, barbecue sauce and pickle relish; micro-cook 10 minutes. Stir. For each sandwich, top bottom half of bun with process cheese spread and meat mixture. Serve with top half of bun.   8 sandwiches

Denver Delight Sandwich

2 tablespoons Parkay margarine
2 tablespoons chopped green
   pepper
1 tablespoon chopped onion
6 eggs, beaten
1/2 cup chopped cooked ham

1/3 cup milk
Salt and pepper
   *   *   *
6 hamburger buns, split, toasted
Velveeta pasteurized process
   cheese spread, sliced

Combine margarine, green pepper and onion. Micro-cook 1 minute. Add combined eggs, ham, milk and seasonings. Micro-cook 2 1/2 minutes; stir. Micro-cook 1 minute and 15 seconds; stir. Micro-cook additional 1 minute and 15 seconds; stir.

For each sandwich, cover bottom half of bun with process cheese spread; broil until process cheese spread melts. Top with scrambled eggs; serve with top half of bun.   6 sandwiches

Beefy Supper Sandwich

1/4 cup Parkay margarine
1/4 cup flour
Dash of pepper
2 cups milk
1 3-ounce package smoked sliced
   beef, chopped
2 tablespoons chopped pimiento

1 tablespoon chopped fresh
   parsley
   *   *   *
8 white bread slices, toasted
Kraft American Singles
   pasteurized process cheese food

Micro-cook margarine 30 seconds. Blend in flour and pepper. Gradually stir in milk. Micro-cook 2 1/2 minutes; stir well. Micro-cook 7 to 8 minutes or until mixture boils and thickens, stirring after each minute. Stir in meat, pimiento and parsley.

For each sandwich, cover slice of toast with process cheese food; broil until melted. Top with sauce.   8 sandwiches

Monterey Barbecue Sandwiches

1 pound ground beef
1/2 cup chopped onion
1 16-ounce can kidney beans,
   drained
1/2 cup Kraft barbecue sauce
1 teaspoon chili powder

1/2 cup Cheez Whiz pasteurized
   process cheese spread or
   Cheez Whiz with jalapeño
   peppers
6 hamburger buns, split, toasted

Combine meat and onion. Micro-cook 5 minutes; drain. Stir in kidney beans, barbecue sauce and chili powder; micro-cook 7 minutes. Stir in process cheese spread; micro-cook 1 minute. For each sandwich, cover bottom half of bun with meat mixture and top half of bun.   6 sandwiches

Savoy Sandwiches

2 tablespoons Parkay margarine
2 tablespoons chopped green
　pepper
4 eggs, beaten
1/4 teaspoon salt

Dash of pepper
3 English muffins, split, toasted
6 Canadian-style bacon slices,
　cooked
"Philly" Sauce Supreme

Combine margarine and green pepper. Micro-cook 30 seconds. Add combined eggs and seasonings. Micro-cook 1 minute and 45 seconds; stir. Micro-cook 45 seconds. For each sandwich, cover muffin half with bacon and scrambled eggs. Top with "Philly" Sauce Supreme.　6 sandwiches

Broccoli Milanese

"Philly" Sauce Supreme

2 10-ounce packages frozen
　broccoli spears, cooked,
　drained

Pour "Philly" Sauce Supreme over hot broccoli. Sprinkle with parmesan cheese, if desired.　6 to 8 servings

"Philly" Sauce Supreme

1/2 cup milk
1 8-ounce package Philadelphia
　Brand cream cheese, cubed

1/2 teaspoon onion salt
1/4 cup (1 ounce) Kraft grated
　parmesan cheese

Combine milk and cream cheese. Micro-cook 1 minute; stir well. Add remaining ingredients. Micro-cook 1 minute or until cream cheese is melted; stir well.　1 1/2 cups

Ham Cheese Strata

8 white bread slices, crusts
　trimmed
1 8-ounce package Deluxe Choice
　sharp • Old English
　pasteurized process cheese
1 cup chopped ham

4 eggs, beaten
2 cups milk
1/2 teaspoon salt
1/4 teaspoon dry mustard
Dash of pepper

Place 4 slices of bread in bottom of greased 8-inch square baking dish. Cover with 4 cheese slices, ham, remaining cheese slices and remaining bread slices. Combine eggs, milk and seasonings; pour over bread. Cover; refrigerate 1 hour or overnight. Micro-cook 20 minutes, turning half turn every 5 minutes. Let stand a few minutes; cut into squares.　4 servings

Laredo Chili

1 pound ground beef
1 cup chopped tomato
1/2 cup chopped onion
1/2 cup chopped green pepper
2 teaspoons chili powder
1 16-ounce can kidney beans,
   drained

1 8-ounce jar Cheez Whiz
   pasteurized process cheese
   spread or Cheez Whiz
   with jalapeño peppers

Combine meat, tomato, onion, green pepper and chili powder; micro-cook 7 minutes. Stir in kidney beans; micro-cook additional 7 minutes. Stir in process cheese spread. Micro-cook 1 minute or until process cheese spread is melted. Serve with corn chips, if desired.   4 to 6 servings

Three Bean Chili

1 16-ounce can pork and beans
1 16-ounce can kidney beans,
   undrained
1 16-ounce can green beans,
   drained

6 crisply cooked bacon slices,
   coarsely crumbled
1 8-ounce jar Cheez Whiz
   pasteurized process cheese
   spread with jalapeño peppers

Combine beans and bacon. Micro-cook 10 minutes, stirring occasionally. Add process cheese spread; micro-cook 2 minutes. Stir well.   4 to 6 servings

Early Riser's Rabbit

1/2 pound Velveeta pasteurized
   process cheese spread, cubed
1/4 cup milk
1 tablespoon prepared mustard

8 whole wheat bread slices,
   toasted, cut in half diagonally
12 tomato slices

Combine process cheese spread, milk and mustard. Micro-cook 30 seconds; stir well. Micro-cook an additional 30 seconds. Stir until sauce is smooth. For each serving, cover four toast halves with 3 tomato slices. Top with sauce. Sprinkle with crumbled bacon, if desired.   4 servings

---

A liquid mixture heated in a microwave oven should be stirred before serving, to distribute the heat evenly.

Opposite: Laredo Chili

Beef and Noodles Midwestern

1 pound ground beef
1/2 cup chopped onion
2 cups (4 ounces) noodles,
  cooked, drained
1 8-ounce jar Cheez Whiz
  pasteurized process cheese
  spread

1 2 1/2-ounce jar mushrooms,
   drained
1/2 teaspoon salt
1/4 teaspoon pepper
1/4 teaspoon paprika

Combine meat and onion. Micro-cook 5 minutes; drain. Stir in noodles, process cheese spread, mushrooms and seasonings. Micro-cook 4 minutes; stir.   4 servings

As with conventional recipes, the recipes in this chapter should be cooked uncovered unless specific instructions are given to cover during cooking.

Savory Scrambled Eggs

2 tablespoons Parkay margarine
6 eggs, beaten
1/3 cup milk

Salt and pepper
1 3-ounce package Philadelphia
   Brand cream cheese, cubed

Micro-cook margarine 30 seconds. Add remaining ingredients. Micro-cook 2 minutes; stir. Micro-cook additional 4 minutes, stirring occasionally.   4 servings

Dynasty Eggs

2 tablespoons Parkay margarine
2 tablespoons flour
1/2 teaspoon salt
1 1/2 cups milk
4 hard-cooked eggs, quartered
1 6-ounce can water chestnuts,
   drained, sliced

2 tablespoons green onion slices
4 English muffins, split, toasted
Deluxe Choice American
   pasteurized process cheese

Micro-cook margarine 30 seconds. Add flour and salt; gradually stir in milk. Micro-cook 2 1/2 minutes or until mixture boils and thickens, stirring occasionally. Add eggs, water chestnuts and onion; micro-cook 1 minute. For each serving, cover muffin half with cheese; micro-cook 45 seconds or until cheese begins to melt. Top with egg mixture.   8 servings

Noodle 'n Frank Dinner

1 pound frankfurters, sliced
1 pound Velveeta pasteurized
    process cheese spread, cubed
1/2 cup milk

4 cups (8 ounces) noodles,
    cooked, drained
1 teaspoon parsley flakes

Micro-cook frankfurters 5 minutes. Add process cheese spread and milk; micro-cook 2 minutes, stirring once. Add noodles and parsley. Micro-cook 1 minute; stir.   6 servings

Refer to the "Use and Care Booklet" that comes with your microwave oven for information on recommended cooking equipment and more exact information on the amount of time required to cook food in *your* oven.

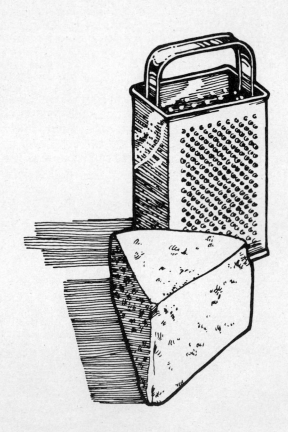

Microwave ovens vary from one model to the next. Therefore the recipes given in this chapter may require slight adjustments in cooking time.

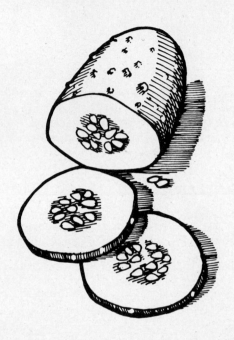

Alpine Fondue

1 6-ounce package Kraft shredded
 natural Swiss cheese
2 tablespoons flour
1 garlic clove, cut in half

3/4 cup dry white wine
Salt and pepper
1 tablespoon Kirsch
French or Vienna bread chunks

Toss cheese and flour together. Rub inside of 1 1/2-quart casserole with garlic; pour in wine. Cover; micro-cook 1 minute. Add half the cheese mixture; stir well. Micro-cook 1 minute. Stir in remaining cheese mixture; micro-cook 1 minute. Stir well. Stir in seasonings and Kirsch. Micro-cook 30 seconds. Pour fondue into fondue pot; keep warm while serving. If fondue becomes too thick, pour in a little warmed wine. Serve with bread.   3 to 4 servings

Saucy Chicken

1/2 cup celery slices
1/4 cup chopped onion
1/4 cup chopped green pepper
1/4 cup Parkay margarine
3 tablespoons flour
3/4 cup milk
1 8-ounce jar Cheez Whiz
   pasteurized process cheese
   spread or Cheez Whiz with
   pimento

1 2 1/2-ounce jar mushrooms,
   drained
1/3 cup slivered almonds, toasted
2 cups chopped cooked chicken
Toast or biscuits

Combine celery, onion, green pepper and margarine; micro-cook
1 1/2 minutes. Blend in flour. Gradually stir in milk. Micro-cook
2 1/2 minutes or until mixture boils and thickens. Add remaining ingredients. Micro-cook 5 minutes; stir. Serve over toast.
6 servings

Southern-Style Creamed Chicken

1/2 cup chopped onion
3 tablespoons Parkay margarine
2 tablespoons flour
1/2 teaspoon salt
Dash of cayenne
1 1/2 cups milk
1 1/2 cups (6 ounces) shredded
   Kraft sharp natural cheddar
   cheese

1/4 cup Kraft real mayonnaise
1 1/2 cups chopped cooked chicken
1 10-ounce package frozen peas,
   cooked, drained
4 hard-cooked eggs, sliced
1 4-ounce jar mushrooms, drained
6 corn bread squares

Combine onion and margarine; micro-cook 1 minute. Blend in flour
and seasonings. Gradually stir in milk. Micro-cook 2 1/2 minutes or
until sauce boils and thickens. Add cheese. Micro-cook 1 1/2
minutes. Stir in mayonnaise. Add chicken, peas, eggs and mushrooms. Micro-cook 4 minutes. Serve over corn bread.   6 servings

Cheese should always be melted in as short a time as possible. Small portions of food covered with cheese, such as a piece of pie or a hamburger, require only about 15 seconds to melt the cheese. It may take as long as a minute to melt cheese on a casserole.

Quick Rabbit Supper

1 8-ounce jar Cheez Whiz
   pasteurized process cheese
   spread

8 tomato slices
4 white bread slices, toasted
8 crisply cooked bacon slices

Remove jar lid from process cheese spread. Micro-cook 30 seconds; stir. Micro-cook 45 seconds. For each serving, place 2 tomato slices on slice of toast. Top with process cheese spread and bacon.   4 servings

Broccoli and Corn Scallop

2 tablespoons chopped onion
Parkay margarine
1 tablespoon flour
1 1/4 cups milk
1 8-ounce package shredded
  Casino brand natural monterey
  jack cheese

1 12-ounce can whole kernel
  corn, drained
1/2 cup cracker crumbs
2 10-ounce packages frozen
  broccoli spears, cooked, drained

Combine onion and 1 tablespoon margarine; micro-cook 1 minute. Blend in flour. Gradually stir in milk. Micro-cook 2 1/2 minutes or until sauce boils and thickens. Stir in cheese; micro-cook 1 minute. Stir in corn and 1/4 cup crumbs. Arrange broccoli in 11 3/4 x 7 1/2-inch baking dish. Pour cheese sauce over broccoli. Toss remaining crumbs with 1 tablespoon melted margarine; sprinkle over casserole. Micro-cook 5 minutes; turn 1/2 turn. Micro-cook additional 5 minutes.   8 servings

Opposite: Spaghetti Special (page 184), Frozen Chocolate Delight (page 184)

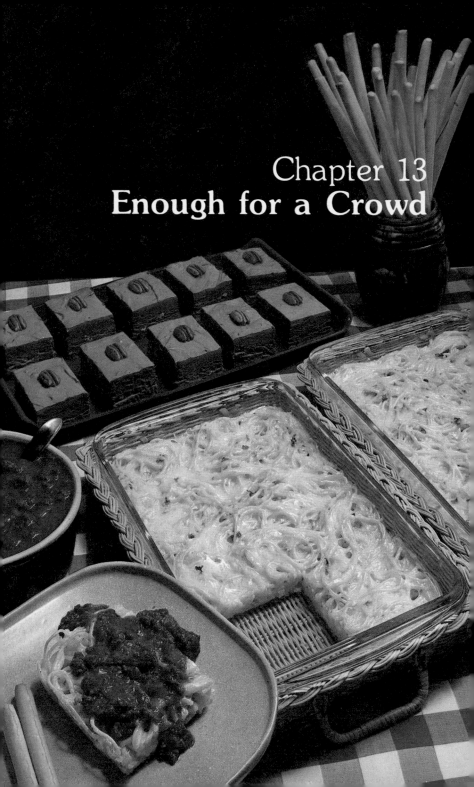

Chapter 13
Enough for a Crowd

Spaghetti Special

14 ounces spaghetti, cooked,
    drained
4 eggs, beaten
1/2 cup (2 ounces) Kraft grated
    parmesan cheese
1/4 cup parsley flakes
2 8-ounce packages Kraft shredded
    natural low moisture part-skim
    mozzarella cheese

        *   *   *
1 pound ground beef
1 cup chopped celery
2 6-ounce cans tomato paste
2 cups water
1 teaspoon salt
1/2 teaspoon celery salt
1/2 teaspoon oregano
1/2 teaspoon garlic powder

Combine spaghetti, eggs, parmesan cheese and parsley. In two greased 11 3/4 x 7 1/2-inch baking dishes, layer half of spaghetti mixture and mozzarella cheese; repeat layers. Bake at 350°, 20 minutes.

Brown meat; drain. Add celery; cook until celery is tender. Stir in tomato paste, water and seasonings. Simmer 15 minutes, stirring occasionally. Cut baked spaghetti into squares; serve with sauce. 16 servings

Frozen Chocolate Delight

2 cups graham cracker crumbs
1/3 cup granulated sugar
1/2 cup Parkay margarine, melted
1 1-ounce square unsweetened
    chocolate, melted
        *   *   *
2 8-ounce packages Philadelphia
    Brand cream cheese

1 1/2 cups packed brown sugar
1/2 teaspoon peppermint extract
2 6-ounce packages semi-sweet
    chocolate pieces, melted
3 eggs, separated
1 cup heavy cream, whipped
1 cup chopped pecans

Combine crumbs and sugar; stir in margarine and chocolate. Press onto bottom of 13 x 9-inch baking pan; chill.

Combine softened cream cheese, 1 1/4 cups brown sugar and extract, mixing until well blended. Blend in chocolate and egg yolks. Beat egg whites until soft peaks form. Gradually add remaining sugar, beating until stiff peaks form. Fold egg whites, whipped cream and nuts into cream cheese mixture. Pour over crust; freeze until firm, several hours or overnight. 20 servings

---

Add color and flavor to a meal by topping slices of tomato with a mixture of grated parmesan cheese tossed with bread crumbs and melted margarine. Broil before serving.

Remember, when a recipe is doubled or tripled, spices and seasoning may have to be adjusted in order to avoid an overpowering flavor in the finished dish.

Chicken Spaghetti

2/3 cup Parkay margarine
2/3 cup flour
12 cups milk
2 teaspoons salt
1 teaspoon garlic powder
1 teaspoon onion salt
1/2 teaspoon pepper
3 cups (12 ounces) Kraft grated
  parmesan cheese

2 pounds spaghetti, broken
  in half, cooked, drained
3 cups chopped cooked chicken
1/2 cup chopped fresh parsley
1 4-ounce jar pimiento, drained,
  chopped

Make a white sauce with margarine, flour, milk and seasonings in a 2-gallon pot. Stir in cheese. Add remaining ingredients; mix thoroughly. Heat.   24 1-cup servings

Jubilee Corn

1 cup chopped onion
1/2 cup Parkay margarine
1/2 cup flour
3/4 pound Velveeta pasteurized
  process cheese spread, cubed

3 cups chopped tomatoes
3 16-ounce cans whole kernel
  corn, drained
1 teaspoon salt
Dash of pepper

In a Dutch oven, sauté onion in margarine; blend in flour. Stir in process cheese spread and tomatoes. Cook until process cheese spread melts. Add corn and seasonings. Heat, stirring constantly.   18 1/2-cup servings

Party Grills

3 9 1/4-ounce cans tuna, drained,
  flaked
4 cups (16 ounces) shredded Kraft
  sharp natural cheddar cheese
1 cup chopped celery
4 hard-cooked eggs, chopped

1/4 cup chopped onion
1 1/2 cups Miracle Whip salad
  dressing
60 white bread slices
Soft Parkay margarine

Combine tuna, cheese, celery, eggs, onion and salad dressing. For each sandwich, cover slice of bread with about 1/3 cup tuna mixture. Top with second slice of bread. Spread bread with margarine. Place sandwiches on cookie sheets; broil on both sides until golden brown.   30 sandwiches

---

Add the zest of grated parmesan cheese to a tossed salad prepared for a large group.

Starboard Bean Salad

2 16-ounce cans cut green
  beans, drained
2 16-ounce cans lima beans,
  drained
2 16-ounce cans kidney beans,
  drained

1 cup chopped tomato
1/2 cup celery slices
4 cups (16 ounces) cubed Kraft
  sharp natural cheddar cheese
1 8-ounce bottle Catalina brand
  French dressing

Combine vegetables and cheese. Add dressing; toss. Chill.
20 3/4-cup servings

Cover pieces of sheet cake with whipped cream cheese and butterscotch topping to make a simple but attractive dessert.

Tuna Bake

9 cups cooked rice
1 cup chopped onion
2 12-ounce cans tuna, drained,
   flaked
2 10-ounce packages frozen peas,
   thawed
2 10 3/4-ounce cans cream of
   mushroom soup, undiluted

1 cup milk
1 1/2 teaspoons Worcestershire
   sauce
2 pounds Velveeta pasteurized
   process cheese spread
4 cups crushed potato chips

Combine rice, onion, tuna, peas, soup, milk, Worcestershire sauce
and 1 1/2 pounds process cheese spread, cubed. Spoon into two
13 1/2 x 8 3/4-inch baking dishes; sprinkle with potato chips. Bake
at 350°, 30 minutes. Top with remaining process cheese spread,
sliced; continue baking until process cheese spread melts.
16 3/4-cup servings

Praline Cheese Dessert

1 1/2 cups graham cracker crumbs
3 tablespoons granulated sugar
3 tablespoons Parkay margarine,
    melted

*   *   *

4 8-ounce packages Philadelphia
    Brand cream cheese

1 1/2 cups packed dark brown
    sugar
3 tablespoons flour
4 eggs
2 teaspoons vanilla
3/4 cup finely chopped pecans

Combine crumbs, sugar and margarine and press onto bottom of
13 x 9-inch baking pan. Bake at 350°, 10 minutes.

Combine softened cream cheese, brown sugar and flour, mixing
at medium speed on electric mixer until well blended. Add eggs,
one at a time, mixing well after each addition. Blend in vanilla and
nuts. Pour mixture over crumbs. Bake at 350°, 35 to 40 minutes or
until knife inserted 1 inch in from edge comes out clean. Chill.
Brush with maple syrup before serving, if desired.
20 to 24 servings

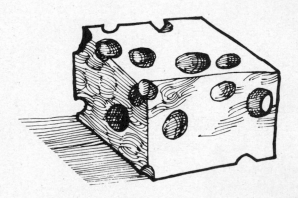

Frankfurter Potato Casserole

2 16-ounce jars Cheez Whiz
    pasteurized process cheese
    spread
1 cup milk
12 cups cooked potato slices

2 pounds frankfurters, cut
    into 1-inch pieces
2 10-ounce packages frozen peas,
    thawed

Heat process cheese spread and milk over low heat; stir until
smooth. Spoon combined potatoes, frankfurters and peas into two
13 1/2 x 8 3/4-inch baking dishes; top with sauce. Cover with
aluminum foil; bake at 350°, 45 minutes.   20 1-cup servings

Confetti Potatoes

6 cups hot mashed potatoes
3 cups (12 ounces) shredded Kraft
   sharp natural cheddar cheese
1/2 cup chopped pimiento

3 tablespoons freeze-dried chives
2 teaspoons salt
1/4 teaspoon pepper
4 medium tomatoes, sliced

Combine potatoes, 2 cups cheese, pimiento, chives and seasonings. Spoon into two greased 13 x 9-inch baking pans. Bake at 350°, 25 minutes. Top with tomato slices and remaining cheese. Continue baking until cheese melts. 18 1/2-cup servings

---

You can stretch a small quantity of meat by adding cheese to the recipe.

Super Scrambled Eggs

3/4 cup Parkay margarine
36 eggs, beaten
2 cups milk
2 teaspoons salt
1/2 teaspoon pepper

2 8-ounce packages Philadelphia
   Brand cream cheese, cubed
1 pound crisply cooked bacon
   slices, crumbled

Melt half of margarine in each of two 10-inch skillets. Combine eggs, milk and seasonings; add half of egg mixture to each skillet. Cook slowly, stirring until eggs begin to thicken. Add half of cream cheese and bacon to each skillet; continue cooking, stirring occasionally, until cheese is melted and eggs are cooked.   24 servings

Merry Cranberry Freeze

6 cups cranberries, ground or
  finely chopped
3 cups sugar
2 8 1/4-ounce cans crushed
  pineapple, undrained

1 cup chopped walnuts
2 8-ounce packages Philadelphia
  Brand cream cheese
2 cups heavy cream, whipped

Combine cranberries and sugar; stir in pineapple and nuts. Gradually add mixture to softened cream cheese, mixing until well blended. Fold in whipped cream. Pour into two 13 x 9-inch baking pans; freeze.   24 servings

Opposite: Cheese and Wine Party Setting (page 197)

Chapter 14
Perfect Partners
— Cheese and Wine

Cheese and wine are natural and delightful partners. Both need aging and both are among the oldest foods known and enjoyed by man.

Many cheeses and wines originated in small villages a long time ago, and in many instances both outstripped their origins in fame and popularity. Champagne and the Roquefort cheese of France are good examples. Today, champagne, the popular sparkling white wine, is produced around the world. Roquefort, the blue-veined cheese made from sheep's milk, was the forerunner of the world-famous blue cheese, now made throughout the United States and Europe.

When cheese and wine are served together the flavor of each is enhanced. Wine tasting parties are becoming increasingly popular as a way to entertain. But a wine tasting party without cheese is like corned beef without cabbage. The combination of cheese and wine can turn an ordinary picnic into a memorable outing, a simple dinner party into an elegant meal, and a dinner for two into a really special occasion.

But not every cheese goes with every wine, so we've made some suggestions in this chapter to help you mix and match. The more cheeses and wines you become familiar with, the more easily you will be able to make your own combinations.

A SHORT GUIDE TO WINE

Both cheese and wine are classified by taste and texture. While cheese is divided into nine basic families, wine can be more or less categorized into six groups.

Appetizer wines are usually dry and served before a meal. Serve chilled, at room temperature, or over ice. Sherry and vermouth are representative of this group.

Dessert wines are sweet, rich wines, usually served in the late afternoon, after dinner or with dessert. Serve them at room temperature. Cream sherry, Madeira, port and muscatel types are typical dessert wines.

Sparkling wines are festive wines, appropriate at any time. They range in taste from very dry to sweet, and should be served well-chilled. Champagne, Sparkling Burgundy, Sparkling Muscat and Crackling Rosé are examples.

White wines, pale golden or green-gold in color, are served chilled. (They should be refrigerated for one hour.) Whites range from light, medium dry wines like Chablis and Dry Sauterne to crisp, dry wines like Riesling and Traminer. Gewürztraminer is a light wine with a hint of spiciness. Full-flavored and rich white wines include such favorites as Pinot Chardonnay, Dry Semillon and Sauvignon Blanc.

Rosé wines are delicate pink or orange-pink in color. They are light and fruity and range from dry to slightly sweet. Serve chilled, like white wines. Grenache Rosé, Cabernet Rosé and Gamay Rosé are examples, named for the grapes from which they are made.

Red wines vary. Lighter reds are fresh and fruity, dry and light to medium in body. The rich, ruby-colored reds with full flavor are the aristocrats — perfect with sharp cheese. Open them an hour before serving to allow the wine to "breathe." The Bordeaux clarets and Burgundy reds are frequently named for the districts which produce them — Margaux, St. Emilion, Médoc, Pomerol, and Côte de Beaune, Beaujolais, etc. Other reds, "varietels," are named for the grapes from which they are made, such as Cabernet, Pinot Noir, Zinfandel and Barbera.

HOW TO TASTE WINE

Pour a small portion (about an ounce) of wine into a clear glass. An all-purpose wine glass with an 8 to 9-ounce capacity is best. Hold the glass up to the light so you can admire the color of the wine, swirl the wine gently in the glass to release the bouquet, then sniff. Now taste it, a small sip at a time. Roll it around your tongue so you can taste the wine fully. Then swallow and you will be able to savor an additional taste sensation. Clear your palate with unsalted crackers, melba toast, bread sticks or French bread, along with some cheese, before you taste another sample of wine. Be sure to use a clean glass.

WHAT WINE GOES WITH WHAT CHEESE?

According to some experts, a red wine is the best wine to serve with most kinds of cheese. But you should suit your own taste. At one time there was a great deal of mystique surrounding the buying, serving and drinking of wine. Each wine had to be served in the "proper" glass, and the various wines were served in a prescribed order throughout a meal that often included as many as seven wines to accompany as many different courses.

Times and customs have changed and, happily, you are able to let your taste be your guide when choosing a cheese and selecting a wine to go with it. Variously shaped wine glasses are still used, but many people serve all kinds of wine in a simple, all-purpose, tulip-shaped stemmed glass.

GOOD TASTE, GOOD SENSE

A simple rule for choosing cheese and wine that go together is to trust yourself and use common sense. It's very unlikely you'll decide to serve Limburger or Lager Käse with champagne, or, at the other extreme, cream cheese and fresh strawberries with a young, harsh Chianti. In between such limits of absurdity you can let your own taste and good sense tell you what goes with what.

To help you get started on your cheese-and-wine planning, here are some combinations that have a particular affinity.

Camembert: Try a hearty red wine — perhaps a Pinot Noir, any of the other Burgundies, or a Cabernet Sauvignon. This lovely, creamy cheese may also be served for dessert with crackers and/or fruit and, of course, with a sweet dessert wine.

Swiss and Gruyère: The sweet, nutlike flavor of these cheeses goes well with a white table wine — a Chablis or Sauterne perhaps, one of the Rhine wines, or any of the fine American white wines. Champagne also goes well with these cheeses.

Roquefort and Blue: Sharp and tangy in flavor, these cheeses, with their handsome blue-green veins, make perfect partners for sturdy red wines. Try a good, robust Burgundy, an elegant Bordeaux claret, or one of their American cousins. Or, for a change, try a nutty dry sherry.

All the Cheddars: These cheeses range in flavor from mild to extra sharp. California's great Zinfandel, or any rosé wine, goes well with most Cheddars. With the sharpest Cheddars, choose a Burgundy, perhaps a Beaujolais or a sturdy Italian Chianti.

Provolone and Mozzarella: Both of these cheeses are soft, mild and smooth, although provolone usually has a smoky flavor. Good Italian Chianti is an excellent choice, but rosé wines and white wines go well with them, too.

Edam and Gouda: The good "cannonball" cheeses are great combined with Cabernet Sauvignon. They do equally well with a sweeter, dessert-type wine such as a rich port.

Cream Cheese and Neufchatel: Creamy and mild in flavor, these cheeses are great favorites, even among those very few people who "don't like cheese!" Serve them with dessert wines, port or cream sherry, or with a sparkling wine.

Brick, Muenster and Monterey Jack: These cheeses are reasonably mild, yet each has a distinctive flavor. Rosé wines complement them beautifully, as does California's Gamay Beaujolais. For a totally different flavor combination, experiment with a white Rhine wine.

CHEESE AND WINE TASTING

Cheese and wine are appropriate for any way you entertain, whether formal or informal. When you select cheese for a tasting party, choose types that offer a variety of flavors, from mild to sharp, as well as a blend of textures, from creamy smooth to firm. You'll find the contrasting colors and shapes of cheeses can be used to create a dramatic effect.

TIPS ON SERVING CHEESE

Temperature: Most cheese should be served at room temperature. For maximum flavor remove cheese from the refrigerator an hour or so before you plan to serve it.

Tasting: The more delicately flavored, mild cheeses should be tasted before the sharper cheeses.

Quantity: Estimate between a quarter and a half pound per person. However, the greater the variety of cheeses you offer, the more you'll need of each cheese, to provide all of your guests with an adequate sampling.

TIPS ON SERVING WINE

Temperature: Different kinds of wine are usually served at different temperatures. In general, appetizer wines, white table wines, roses and sparkling wines are served chilled (an hour in the refrigerator is enough). Red wines are usually served at room temperature, about 65°. They should be opened an hour before serving to allow them to breathe. (You can open the wine at the same time you remove the cheese from the refrigerator.)

Tasting: Pour the wine into clear glasses. Provide a clean glass for each wine, if possible. Otherwise, have a pitcher of water and some arrangement handy for rinsing glasses. Taste dry wines before you taste sweet wines, whites before reds.

Quantity: A fifth of wine (24 ounces) provides about fifteen tastings. A taste of wine is between 1 and 2 ounces; a normal serving is 4 to 6 ounces. Allow a total near one-half bottle per person.

CHEESE AND WINE SAMPLER

A few combinations of cheese and wine are suggested below. It's a good idea to select several combinations for a sampling. Arrange each type of cheese, attractively cut, on a tray or board with bread or crackers, appropriate spreaders and the suggested wine.

Wine	Cheese
Appetizer Wines: Cocktail or Dry sherry	Cream Cheese Cheddar Dip
Dessert Wines: Tawny port Cream sherry	Edam Gouda
Sparkling Wines: Extra dry Champagne	Cream Cheese Balls Rolled in Almonds
White Wines: Johannisberg Riesling Pinot Chardonnay	Swiss Provolone
Rosé Wines: Grenache Rosé Gamay Rosé	Muenster Brick
Red Wines: Gamay Beaujolais Zinfandel Barbera Cabernet Sauvignon Pinot Noir	Monterey Jack Danish Camembert Sharp Natural Cheddar Cheese Blue Roquefort

FESTIVE CHEESE AND WINE SUGGESTIONS

Classic Cheese Tray: Slice off pieces of sharp natural Cheddar, add chunks of natural Swiss, include a midget colby longhorn for shape as well as flavor, then add a colorful round of Edam. Serve with unsalted crackers, rye rounds and melba toast. Garnish with fruit and offer a red wine such as Cabernet Sauvignon or Pinot Noir, and a white wine such as Chablis or Riesling.

Suggested amounts for 16 people: Two 10-ounce packages of Cracker Barrel brand sharp natural cheddar cheese, one pound of Kraft natural Swiss cheese, one 26-ounce round of Kraft natural edam cheese, two 1-pound Kraft midget longhorn style natural colby cheeses, and four bottles each of the red and white wines.

International Sampler: Serve a generous board featuring wedges of blue-veined Roquefort, cubes of sharp natural Cheddar cheese, and a natural Gouda, cut into wedges. Surround with unsalted crackers and French bread. Serve Pinot Noir with the Roquefort and Cheddar, and Cabernet Sauvignon with the Gouda.

Suggested amounts for 12 people: Four 3-ounce wedges of Louis Rigal Roquefort cheese, one 1-pound Kraft gouda cheese, two 10-ounce packages of Cracker Barrel brand sharp natural cheddar cheese, four bottles of Pinot Noir, and three bottles of Cabernet Sauvignon.

Cheese and Fruit Dessert: Center an imported Danish Camembert on an attractive platter, add a block of cream cheese served with currant jelly, some natural blue cheese, and slices of natural brick cheese. Garnish with fresh grapes and include a basket of pears and apples. Accompany with dessert wines such as port and cream sherry.

Suggested amounts for 6 people: One 5 1/4-ounce can of Tiny Dane brand imported Danish Camembert soft ripened cheese, one 8-ounce package Philadelphia Brand cream cheese, one 6-ounce package Casino brand natural blue cheese, one 8-ounce package Casino brand natural brick cheese, two bottles of cream sherry and two bottles of port.

Picnic Board: Pack a picnic basket with a loaf of French bread, sticks of sharp natural Cheddar, Muenster and a ball of Gouda. Bring along Pinot Noir and Gamay Beaujolais.

Suggested amount for 4 people: One 10-ounce stick Cracker Barrel brand sharp natural cheddar cheese, one 8-ounce Kraft gouda cheese, one 8-ounce package Casino brand natural muenster cheese, and one bottle each of Pinot Noir and Gamay Beaujolais.

Informal Cheese Cart: Set out a tea cart or a TV tray arranged with crackers and samplings of natural Swiss cheese, Edam and Monterey Jack cheese. Serve with Johannisberg Riesling and Zinfandel.

Suggested amounts for 8 people: One 12-ounce round Kraft natural edam cheese, 8 ounces Kraft natural Swiss cheese, one 8-ounce package Casino brand natural monterey jack cheese and two bottles each of Johannisberg Riesling and Zinfandel.

Chapter 15
Through the Ages with Cheese

Where did cheese originate? How is cheese made? How many kinds of cheese are there? These, and dozens of other questions about cheese, one of the world's favorite — and most nutritious — foods, are answered here.

Cheese-making has a long history, but its origins are lost in the far reaches of time. The discovery of cheese probably was an accident — as simple an accident as someone tasting curdled milk and finding the taste to his liking. Two legends persist that are worth repeating because, as with many legends, they are interesting and likely stories.

A NEWS-MAKING CAMEL RIDE

The first legend concerns a desert tribesman of long ago who set out on a journey with a container of milk. It probably was mare's or camel's milk, carried in the usual milk container of the period, the dried stomach of a sheep. The tribesman mounted his camel and took off in the broiling desert sun on a ride that was as bumpy and lurchy as a camel ride is to this day.

When the tribesman stopped to refresh himself, he found the milk had separated into a thin, watery substance (whey) and a thickened mass (curds). This separation occurred as a result of the warmth of the day and the churning motion of the ride, helped along by the action of rennet, an enzyme present in the sheep's stomach. He tasted the mass of curds and was delighted. We can imagine that he could hardly wait to get home to share his great discovery with family and friends. Our tribesman had inadvertently discovered how to make cheese.

A SHEPHERD'S FORGOTTEN LUNCH

The second legend is about a herdsman who went out to tend his sheep long, long ago, taking with him a lunch of fresh goat's milk and a chunk of bread. He laid his lunch aside — perhaps in the shade of a tree, or in a cave — to keep the food cool, and went about his business. Something kept him from lunch that day, and for several days thereafter. When he finally got back to it, he found the cheese in a condition he probably thought of as "spoiled." It was veined with blue mold. He tasted the cheese gingerly and, to his surprise, found it delicious. Our herdsman had just tasted the world's first blue-veined cheese.

CHEESE THROUGH THE AGES

However cheese came to be discovered, it has been a nutritious tasty staple for increasing numbers of people for many years. Tablets dating back to 4,000 B.C. testify to the fact that the Sumerians ate cheese. Archeologists have also established the fact that Egyptians and Chaldeans of long ago knew what wonderful food could be made from clabbered milk. The ancient Greeks thought it a fit offering to their gods. David, on his way to deliver cheese to Saul's camp, interrupted his journey to fight the giant Goliath.

Homer sang about cheese. The Greeks fed their athletes cheese and made their wedding cakes with it. The Romans were familiar with many kinds of cheese. Armies, so the old saying goes, travel on their stomachs. And the men of many ancient armies, including those of Julius Caesar and Genghis Khan, carried cheese to sustain them. Visitors to ancient Sicily brought home tales of incredibly delicious cheesecakes. Charlemagne is said to have had a great fondness for Roquefort. When Marco Polo returned from his journeys he told of many wonders, including the many varieties of cheese he had discovered, and the secrets of how to make them.

Indeed, a history of cheese might be said to be a capsule history of the world.

THE THRIFTY DUTCH

An old story is told to demonstrate Dutch thrift and industry describing how, for centuries, women all over Europe sat in their kitchens keeping their hands and feet busy rocking cradles, knitting, spinning and preparing food. But in Holland there was often a wheel of cheese ripening under the seat cushion of each chair as well.

WHY IS IT CALLED CHEESE?

Where did the word *cheese* come from? The Latin word for cheese was *caseus*, and from that root sprang the German *Käse*, Dutch *kaas*, Gaelic *cais*, Welsh *caws*, Portuguese *queijo* and Spanish *queso*. The same root produced the Old English word *cese* and a variation, *cyse*, which evolved into our present-day word *cheese*.

The modern Italian *formaggio* and French *fromage* developed from the Latin *forma*, which had been taken from *formas*, the name given by the ancient Greeks to the wicker basket in which they drained their cheese.

IS IT A CHEESE — OR A PLACE?

Whatever cheese is called, in whatever country, by now there are a great many varieties of cheese in existence. Estimates range from 700 to 2,000 types. France alone claims 500, and some 200 kinds of cheese are made in the United States.

Many cheeses are named after the places in which they are made — or were first made. Cheddar is the name of a village near Bristol, England, where its namesake cheese was first produced. Today the town is still the center of a thriving cheese industry. Limburger is named after Limburg, Belgium. Roquefort is a region in southern France. Parmesan cheese comes from Parma, Italy. An endless number of towns and villages have become famous because of the popularity of a world-famous cheese.

CURDS AND WHEY

Cheese-making may have begun as a happy accident but it has grown into a huge industry. Cheese production today is based on scientific principles, surrounded by strict regulations that control flavor, wholesomeness, uniformity and purity. Nevertheless, the process of cheese-making still begins as it first began, with the separation of milk into curds and whey.

The kind of milk — sheep, buffalo, reindeer, cow or goat — determines the taste and texture of the finished cheese. The differences in cheese come about because of variation in the preparation of curds, the addition of such friendly organisms as bacteria and mold, and the conditions of the curing or ripening process.

Reduced to its simplest definition, natural cheese is the solid or casein portion of milk (curds) which has been separated from the whey. Coagulation is facilitated and controlled by the action of

rennet, lactic acid, or both. There are six basic steps in the manufacture of natural cheese.

Step One — Preparing the milk:
   After fresh milk is received at the cheese factory from farms, it is
scientifically tested and heat treated. The fat content is adjusted
and the milk is then pumped into vats.

Step Two — Adding coloring, starter and rennet:
   Coloring is not used in all types of cheese, but a safe vegetable
coloring is added to milk to make golden-colored cheese. Then the
starter, a pure culture of microorganisms, is added to help firm the
curd particles and to develop the individual characteristics of the
variety of cheese being manufactured. The addition of rennet extract coagulates the milk into a custard-like mass called *curd.*

Step Three — Cutting the curd and cooking:
   After the curd reaches the firmness of custard, it is cut into small
cubes to permit the watery whey to separate. Curds and whey are
then heated to the required temperature for the type of cheese being made. This firms the curd and hastens the separation of whey
from the curd.

Step Four — Draining the whey:
   The whey is removed from the curd by simple drainage or by one
of several mechanical methods.

Step Five — Salting the curd:
   The point at which salt is added, and the amount of salt, have a
definite effect on the type of cheese produced. Sometimes salt is
added after pressing (step 6).

Step Six — Pressing and curing the cheese:
   The salted curd is weighed and pressed into forms to produce a
solid block of cheese. The cheese is then kept in temperature-
controlled storage rooms to cure until the desired texture and
flavor have developed.

CHEESE FAMILIES OR GROUPS
   A specific range of time and temperature, along with specific
conditions of curing, is required for each cured cheese. The result is
the development of a particular type of cheese. Aging may take up
to twelve months — although some cheese is aged for as long as
twenty-four months — depending on the sharpness desired. The
cheese is then cut into portions of convenient size, and packaged in
sealed wrappings to suit popular demand.

Just as there are many nations in the world, there are great families, or related groups, of cheese. All varieties of cheese stem from nine basic families: Cheddar, Dutch, provolone, Swiss, blue, Parmesan, fresh, surface-ripened, and whey. Although most of these cheeses originated in Europe, the cheese we find in supermarkets today may be either imported or domestic.

CHEDDAR CHEESE FAMILY

Cheddar is the most popular cheese in the United States. Like all other varieties of natural cheese, it is made according to the six basic steps. The variation that sets Cheddar apart from other natural cheeses occurs in Step 4. At that point the curd is allowed to knit together, and is turned and piled to expel the whey. This procedure — known as cheddaring — develops Cheddar's characteristic body and texture. The cheese is then fashioned into a flat slab which is "milled" (cut into smaller pieces) and placed in a hoop or mold.

Colby is another member of the Cheddar family. In its production, the curd particles are stirred and are not allowed to knit together. The result is a more open-textured cheese. The drained curd is washed with cool water, which gives Colby a high moisture content and a mild flavor.

Monterey or Monterey Jack was developed by monks in the early days of California's history. This creamy white cheese is similar to Colby, although it has a higher moisture content, a softer consistency, and a more open texture.

THE DUTCH CHEESES

The most popular varieties of cheese from Holland are Edam and Gouda. Both range from semisoft to hard, and both are sweet-curd cheeses made from cows' milk. They have a characteristic milky, nut-like flavor that varies in intensity with the age of the cheese.

In the United States, Edam is sold in the familiar red cannonball-shape, usually weighing from 3/4 pound to 4 1/2 pounds. In Holland, Edam is a natural gold color, and is sold without the waxy red covering.

Gouda comes in one of two shapes: a flattened sphere or a rectangular loaf. In the Netherlands a Gouda may weigh from 6 to 50 pounds. The size most often seen in our supermarkets is the familiar "baby Gouda," weighing a pound or less. Gouda, too, may or may not have a red wax coating.

Special metal or hardwood molds, lined with cheesecloth, are used in the "pressing" step in the manufacture of Edam and Gouda. These molds, which give the cheeses their characteristic shape, consist of a round lower section, perforated for drainage, and a round cover.

Cheeses made by this method may include mixtures of cumin, caraway and other spices. Some examples are noekkelost, Leyden and cuminost.

THE PROVOLONE CHEESES

The provolone family is technically known as pasta filata (spun) cheese. The essential step in the preparation of cheeses from this family occurs after the separation of the curd from the whey. The curd is placed in either hot water or hot whey, and this changes it into a stringy, plastic-like mass. Then the curd is stretched, much the way taffy is stretched, and it is molded into the desired size and shape. Finally it is salted, soaked in brine, and may, or may not, be smoked.

The most popular member of this cheese family is provolone, which is slightly cured and usually smoked. It is a very important ingredient in Italian cooking.

Mozzarella is another member of this cheese family, one that has become very well-known in the United States because of the popularity of pizza. A fresh cheese, originally made from buffalo milk, it originated in Italy, just south of Rome. Buffalo-milk mozzarella is still sold in that area of Italy, but mozzarella cheese is always made from cows' milk in the United States.

Originally, mozzarella was sold and eaten the same day it was made. But with national distribution and commercial sales, this is no longer possible. However, mozzarella still is a fresh, uncured cheese, particularly adaptable for cooking, because it melts into the smooth, stringy mass, desirable for such dishes as pizza and lasagne.

Scamorze cheese is a close relative of mozzarella. Both are fresh, uncured, and mild in flavor.

THE SWISS CHEESES

Swiss cheese is the second most popular variety of cheese sold in the United States, ranking just behind Cheddar. In Switzerland, where it originated, what we think of as Swiss cheese is called Emmentaler, a name also used in the United States.

The distinguishing feature of Swiss cheese is its "eyes," which are holes that develop throughout the cheese during ripening. These holes are the result of propionic acid bacteria that produce carbon dioxide bubbles throughout the body of the cheese. The size of the holes is partially controlled by regulating the temperature and time of ripening. Propionic acid bacteria also produces the characteristic sweet, nut-like flavor of Swiss cheese.

Gruyère is related to Swiss cheese, although the characteristic "eyes" are not as fully developed. A certain amount of surface growth is allowed to take place, resulting in a somewhat sharper flavor. Gruyère cheese is very popular in Europe, but has never gained similar popularity in the United States.

To avoid confusion, cheese buyers should understand that most Gruyère cheese sold in the United States is a pasteurized process cheese, containing Emmentaler and Gruyère. It is usually sold in small individually wrapped wedges and in round or half-round packages. It is not the same as natural Gruyère.

THE BLUE-VEINED CHEESES

The blue-veined cheeses are characterized by the distribution of blue-green mold throughout the cheese, which produces a characteristic piquant flavor. This blue mold is the result of the inoculation of a strain of penicillium mold that grows throughout the body of the cheese.

Almost every cheese-consuming country in the world has developed a blue-veined cheese similar to the blue cheese produced in the United States. The best-known are Italy's Gorgonzola, England's Stilton, France's Roquefort and Denmark's Danablu.

All these blue cheeses, with the exception of Roquefort, are made from cows' milk. Roquefort is produced from sheep's milk in a region in southeastern France and it is cured in caves that are found in that area.

During the manufacture of blue cheeses, a blue-mold powder (penicillium mold) is mixed with the curd, either while it is in the vat, or while it is being placed in molds or hoops. The cheese is held in these hoops for twenty-four hours.

After it is removed from the hoops, the cheese is salted over a period of one week under conditions that simulate the temperature and humidity of the Roquefort caves. About one week after salting, the cheese is mechanically pierced to produce holes that permit the air penetration essential for mold growth. Then the cheese cures for a period of about five months.

THE PARMESAN CHEESES

The members of this hard grating cheese family, primarily associated with Italian cooking, were originally developed in Italy in the vicinity of Parma. They are grated and sprinkled on spaghetti, pizza, minestrone, other soup, tossed salads, and used in baked dishes, such as veal parmigiana and lasagne.

These cheeses are characterized by their hard, granular texture, which makes them ideal for grating. In fact, much of the Parmesan and Romano cheese produced in the United States is sold grated or shredded, in jars or cardboard containers.

Parmesan is the most familiar cheese in this group and perhaps one of the best-known Italian cheeses available in the United States. It is made from a mixture of whole and skim milk and usually is cured for ten to twenty-four months to develop the characteristic texture and piquant flavor.

Romano, the other member of this cheese family so well-known in the United States, originated in the Latium area near Rome. It is very similar to Parmesan cheese and is used in the same way, but it has a sharper, more piquant flavor. Both Parmesan and Romano are excellent "seasoning cheeses."

THE FRESH, UNCURED CHEESES

The making of fresh cheeses does not follow exactly the six major steps of cheese manufacture. Coagulation of the curd is initiated by the addition of a lactic acid starter, with or without a small amount of rennet. Also, as their name implies, these cheeses are not cured, but are sold fresh and have a mild flavor.

Cream cheese is an American original, enjoyed since 1872. It starts as a mixture of milk and cream, pasteurized and coagulated by a starter. Originally the curd was poured into cloth bags and pressed to expel the whey. About 1945, Kraft perfected a method of removing the curd by centrifugal force. This procedure is the one primarily used today. It produces a fine, smooth-bodied cheese that has greater keeping qualities than cheese produced by the "bag method."

Neufchatel is the name of a lower fat product similar to cream cheese. Because of their mild flavor and smooth creamy texture, both cream cheese and Neufchatel blend readily with other ingredients and are used in a wide variety of recipes. They are especially popular as a base for many dips and spreads.

Cottage cheese is a third member of the family of fresh, uncured cheeses. To make cottage cheese, skim milk is coagulated by adding lactic acid starter and, sometimes, a small amount of rennet. When the curd is sufficiently firm, it is cut into cubes and heated in the whey. After the whey has been removed, the curd is washed and salted. Cottage cheese is usually creamed to improve its flavor and texture. This is done by adding a mixture of cream and milk. Cottage cheese can be purchased in small or large curd form.

THE SURFACE-RIPENED CHEESES

Members of the surface-ripened cheese family include Camembert, Brie, Bel Paese, Port du Salut and Limburger. Brick and Muenster originally were members of this family of cheeses, but they no longer can be considered true members because they have little or no surface ripening today. This is the result of consumer preference for milder and milder versions of these cheeses.

Surface-ripened cheeses are divided into two major groups, based upon the type of organisms used to produce characteristic flavors. In all surface-ripened cheeses a bacterial culture, or a mold culture, is grown on the surface of the cheese. The enzymes produced by the growth of these organisms penetrate the cheese and bring about the development of the particular flavor and texture of each variety.

The two basic sub-families within this large group of cheeses are differentiated by the type of organism used for ripening — mold or bacteria. Camembert and Brie are characteristic of the mold-ripened varieties. Both originated in France and both are very popular with cheese connoisseurs all over the world. The best-known variety of bacterial-ripened cheese is Limburger. Other popular cheeses of this type are Bel Paese of Italy and Port du Salut of France.

THE WHEY CHEESES

The whey group of cheeses is produced from whey rather than curd. They are not true cheeses, because whey is a by-product of the manufacture of cheese.

Whey cheeses vary greatly in characteristics. Perhaps the best-known cheese in this category is ricotta, used frequently in Italian cooking. Ricotta was originally produced by coagulation of the albumen portion of the whey, which produced a soft, fresh cheese similar to cottage cheese. Today, ricotta is made by the coagulation of a mixture of whey and whole or skim milk. It is a soft, grainy cheese, and can be purchased either dry or moist.

Two other cheeses in this family, gjetost and primost, are Scandinavian. They are prepared by condensing whey and adding small amounts of fat. Gjetost is rather hard; primost is a semisoft product. Another member of the family is sapsago, a Swiss type of whey cheese. It is made by the acid coagulation of the protein in a mixture of skim milk, buttermilk and whey. The addition of the leaves of a cloverlike plant leads to the characteristic flavor and light green color. A hard cheese, it is primarily used grated.

See The Cheese Families Charts, pages 214-217.

CHOOSING A FAVORITE CHEESE

Most members of the nine cheese families can be found in the dairy case of your supermarket. By browsing through the recipes in this book you will find interesting and unusual ways to use many of the kinds of cheese available for you and your family to enjoy.

On the following pages there are see-at-a-glance charts that will help you identify the cheeses in the nine families, and which, we hope, will persuade you to buy and experiment with unfamiliar varieties of cheese.

CHEESE BEGINNINGS IN AMERICA

Cheese-making started in this country soon after the Pilgrims landed at Plymouth Rock — in 1624, to be exact. It began immediately after the colonists, sick of their scant and tiresome diet, joyously welcomed the first cows to arrive in the new land.

In 1801, President Thomas Jefferson was presented with a mammoth 1,235-pound cheese. Awe of that monster cheese was responsible for the catch-phrase "big cheese." In those days cheese was usually made at home or on the farm. But gradually a few cheese factories were established. One of the first was a Cheddar factory, built by Jesse Williams in 1851, in Oneida, New York.

As the manufacture of cheese developed and grew into a thriving industry in the United States, it was usual for the producer, or sometimes a wholesaler, to take his cheese to a market in a central location. Almost all cities had large outdoor or indoor markets, where a retailer would come and choose those products he wanted to sell in his store.

YOUNG MAN WITH AN IDEA

In 1903, a young man named James L. Kraft had an idea: Why not take the cheese to the retailer, instead of making the retailer come to the cheese? He had, to begin with, a horse (his name was Paddy), a wagon, and working capital of sixty-five dollars. He also had abounding energy and a boundless imagination. J. L. filled his wagon with cheese at the market, clucked to Paddy, and started making the rounds of Chicago grocers to sell them cheese.

But habit-bound Chicago grocers were unimpressed. They wiped their hands on their long white aprons, twisted the ends of their handlebar moustaches and said, "Well, I don't know . . ."

Some days the total sales added up to less than ten dollars. On such days, J. L. held "business conferences" with Paddy, who gave an occasional twitch of his ears in reply.

One day J. L. explained to Paddy that they had been careless and forgetful. "From now on, Paddy," he told his horse, "we're going to work with God as our Partner."

BUSINESS BEGINS TO IMPROVE

With his wagon hitched to this star, business began to improve, and J. L. and Paddy became the historic "co-founders" of the Kraft Foods Company.

In August of 1904, J. L. wrote to a friend: "To give you an idea of what you would have to do should things work out all right: It is simply a grocery route on a large scale. You take a horse and wagon (and my wagons are fancy ones) and get customers that you can call on once or twice a week and supply them regularly. I am driving one wagon myself, and I am taking care of the horses myself, but if all goes well, I think I will have four horses by Christmas . . ."

As time went on, J. L.'s business flourished and prospered. Not only did he do well, but he learned a great deal about cheese. He learned, for example, that there were problems in the manufacture and distribution of cheese. Many of the problems were connected with the keeping qualities of cheese. Natural cheese has a longer life — both in the store and in the home — than, for instance, the milk from which it is made. It is, however, perishable in degrees that vary with the kind of cheese. The ripening processes that produce the different varieties, textures and flavors of natural cheese don't stop when a particular cheese has reached its prime. In due course deterioration and drying will set in.

In addition to these problems, variations in the handling and curing of cheese cause appreciable differences in taste and texture. In other words, two cheeses of the same brand, same variety, and same age might not necessarily be the same.

J. L. BUYS A DOUBLE BOILER

There ought to be some way to lick these problems, James Kraft decided. Shortly thereafter he found himself in the cheese-making, as well as the cheese-marketing, business. He began to experiment in an ordinary kitchen double boiler (price, fifty-nine cents). He experimented with blended cheeses, and later with the pasteurizing and blending of cheese in an effort to find solutions to these difficulties. There were early failures but, eventually, success. In 1916, the method of producing process cheese was patented by J. L. Kraft.

By 1917, Kraft cheese in tins, a pasteurized process product, was ready for the market. By 1920, Kraft's five-pound loaf, a pasteurized, blended cheese in a wooden container, was placed on sale, and became an immediate, spectacular success.

PASTEURIZED PROCESS CHEESE PRODUCTS

Process cheese is a product manufactured from natural cheese, according to specified government standards. It has had a major influence on the eating habits of the nation.

The processing of natural cheese provides a stable product with great uniformity of flavor and texture. Processing consists of blending various natural cheeses — mild, sharp and extra sharp — by heating them with an emulsifier. The result is a homogeneous product, consistent in flavor, body and texture.

The manufacture of process cheese is quality-controlled throughout to insure uniform good flavor, smooth texture, melting properties and high nutrition. Available in a variety of types, shapes and flavors, process cheese can be counted on to give excellent results in cooking.

The most well-known natural cheeses used for processing are Cheddar and Swiss. There is often some confusion about the differences in various process cheese products — pasteurized process *cheese*, cheese *food* and cheese *spread*. The major differences in these products are shown in this chart:

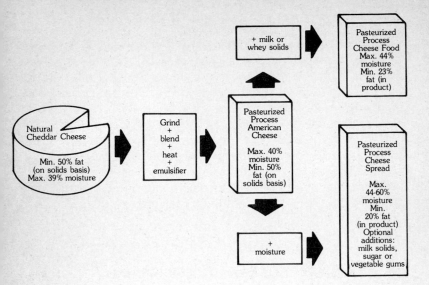

PASTEURIZED PROCESS CHEESE

Natural cheese is always used to start processed cheese products. Natural cheeses of various ages and characteristics are selected, and laboratory tested, to assure the desired quality in the finished process cheese. Grinding or blending of the cheese by machine follows; the blend is then transferred to the cooker.

Emulsifiers, designated to meet established government standards, are added during cooking. Emulsifiers prevent separation of the fat during processing, and produce a cheese with the proper melting and slicing properties.

Pasteurization in the manufacture of process cheese, as in the case of milk, consists of the application of heat. Following established standards, the cheese is pasteurized at a temperature of not less than 150°F for at least thirty seconds. This step prevents further aging of the natural cheeses.

Packing is the final step. The hot, smooth, semi-liquid cheese flows from the cooker to a filling machine, where precisely weighed amounts are poured into containers, lined with moisture-proof material, to form loaves. To make packaged slices, the cheese is run over chilled rollers where it is formed into ribbons of uniform width. These ribbons are run onto a conveyor where they are stacked, cut, and packaged in one continuous operation.

PASTEURIZED PROCESS CHEESE FOOD

Some nutrients of milk remain in the whey when it is drained from the curd during the making of a natural cheese. These nutrients can be returned to the hot cheese during the pasteurization operation. They usually are added in the form of concentrates or powders of skim milk and whey. When these milk solids are added to process cheese, the amount of fat is reduced and the moisture content is increased. The product then becomes pasteurized process *cheese food*. Additional ingredients, such as meat, vegetables and fruit, may be added for variety.

Pasteurized process cheese foods are milder in flavor, and melt more readily, than either natural or pasteurized process cheese.

PASTEURIZED PROCESS CHEESE SPREAD

When a softer, more spreadable cheese product is desired, other ingredients, such as milk products, sweetening agents or vegetable gums, may be added to the process cheese. These products normally have a somewhat higher moisture content and lower fat content than pasteurized process cheese and pasteurized process cheese food. They are referred to as pasteurized process *cheese spreads*. Again, as with cheese foods, other ingredients, such as pimiento, olives, peppers, spices and flavoring may be added to broaden the flavor range.

ADVENTURES IN THE WORLD OF CHEESE

A taste tour of the fascinating world of cheese begins at the dairy case in your neighborhood supermarket. Cheese products, developed through centuries of tradition, are readily available, and offer a vast array of tastes and textures for you to sample. With flavors that run the gamut of mild to sharp, and textures that range from soft and smooth to hard and coarse, there are cheeses to suit every palate.

Cheese provides eating enjoyment and menu variety, two excellent reasons for making cheese important in your meal planning and the preparation of snacks.

DISCOVERING YOUR FAVORITES

With all the varieties of cheese available — over 2,000, according to some dairy scientists — how do you find the ones you and your family will like best? Be adventurous! Try new varieties. Sample cheeses you've heard about, but have never tasted. Introduce your family to different varieties in daily menus. Browse at the dairy case in your supermarket and become familiar with the many kinds of cheese available. Notice, too, the convenient forms in which cheese is sold — slices, sticks, wedges, shredded and grated, all available to help you create dishes that will have the family asking for seconds.

Cheese is unique in its versatility. No other food product is so completely appropriate at any time during a meal, or at any meal during the day. It is both company fare and an important part of the family's diet. It appeals to almost everyone — the young and the old, rich and poor, cheeseburger fans and soufflé-lovers. And speaking of lovers, one can only wonder how Omar Khayyam neglected to include cheese in his immortal paradise of "a loaf of bread, a jug of wine and thou."

The Cheese Families

	CHEESE	ORIGIN	CONSISTENCY AND TEXTURE	COLOR, SHAPE AND FLAVOR	BASIC INGREDIENT	RIPENING PERIOD
Cheddar Family	Cheddar	England	Hard; smooth, firm body	Light yellow to orange; varied shapes and styles with rind and rindless; mild to sharp	Cows' milk, whole	2-12 months or longer
	Colby	United States	Hard type, but softer and more open in texture than Cheddar	Light yellow to orange; cylindrical; mild	Cows' milk, whole	1-3 months
	Monterey (Jack)	United States	Semisoft; smooth, open texture	Creamy white wheels; mild	Cows' milk, whole	2-6 weeks for table use, 6-9 for grating
Dutch Family	Edam	Holland	Hard type, but softer than Cheddar; more open, mealy body	Creamy yellow with or without red wax coat; cannonball shape; mild, nutlike	Cows' milk, partly skimmed	2 months or longer
	Gouda	Holland	Hard type, but softer than Cheddar; more open, mealy body, like Edam	Creamy yellow with or without red wax coat; round and flat, mild; nutlike, similar to Edam	Cows' milk; partly skimmed but more milk fat than Edam	2-6 months
Provolone Family	Provolone	Italy	Hard; compact, flaky	Light golden yellow to golden brown, shiny surface bound with cord; yellowish white interior; pear, sausage and salami shapes; mild to sharp and piquant, usually smoked	Cows' milk, whole	2-12 months
	Mozzarella	Italy	Semisoft; plastic	Creamy white; rectangular and spherical; mild, delicate	Cows' milk, whole or partly skimmed	Unripened
	Scamorze	Italy	Semisoft; Smooth	Light yellow; mild	Cows' milk, whole	Unripened

214

	CHEESE	ORIGIN	CONSISTENCY AND TEXTURE	COLOR, SHAPE AND FLAVOR	BASIC INGREDIENT	RIPENING PERIOD
Swiss Family	Swiss	Switzerland	Hard; smooth with large gas holes, or eyes	Rindless blocks and large wheels with rind; sweetish, nutlike	Cows' milk, partly skimmed	2 months minimum to 9 months or longer
	Gruyere	Switzerland	Hard; tiny gas holes, or eyes	Light yellow; flat wheels; sweetish, nutlike	Cows' milk, usually partly skimmed	3 months minimum
Blue Family	Blue	France	Semisoft; visible veins of mold; pasty, sometimes crumbly	White, marbled with blue-green mold; cylindrical; piquant, spicy	Cows' milk, whole	2 months minimum; 3-4 months usually; 9 months for pronounced flavor
	Gorgonzola	Italy	Semisoft; visible veins of mold; less moist than blue	Light tan surface, light yellow interior, marbled with blue-green mold; cylindrical; piquant, spicy, similar to blue	Cows' milk, whole, or goats' milk or mixture of these	3 months minimum
	Roquefort	France	Semisoft; visible veins of mold; pasty and sometimes crumbly	White marbled with blue-green mold; cylindrical; sharp, piquant, spicy	Sheep's milk	2 months minimum to 5 months or longer
	Stilton	England	Semisoft; visible veins of mold; slightly more crumbly than blue	White, marbled with blue-green mold; cylindrical; piquant, spicy, but milder than Roquefort	Cows' milk, whole with added cream	2-6 months or longer

	CHEESE	ORIGIN	CONSISTENCY AND TEXTURE	COLOR, SHAPE AND FLAVOR	BASIC INGREDIENT	RIPENING PERIOD
Parmesan Family	Parmesan (Reggiano)	Italy	Hard grating; granular, brittle body	Light yellow with brown or black coating; cylindrical; sharp, piquant	Cows' milk, partly skimmed	14 months minimum to 24 months or longer
	Romano	Italy	Hard; granular	Yellowish white interior, greenish black surface; sharp, piquant	Cows' milk	5 months minimum; 12 months for grating
Fresh, Uncured Family	Cream	United States	Soft; smooth, buttery	White; foil-wrapped in rectangular portions; mild, slightly acid	Cream and cows' milk, whole	Unripened
	Neufchatel	France	Soft; smooth, creamy	White; foil-wrapped in rectangular portions; mild	Cows' milk, whole	Unripened
	Cottage	Uncertain	Soft; moist, delicate, large or small curds	White; packaged in cuplike containers; mild, slightly acid	Cows' milk, skimmed; cream dressing may be added	Unripened
Surface-Ripened Family	Camembert	France	Soft; thin edible crust, creamy interior	White crust, creamy yellow interior; small wheels; mild to pungent	Cows' milk, whole	4-5 weeks
	Brie	France	Soft; thin edible crust, creamy interior	Whitish crust, creamy yellow interior; medium and small wheels; mild to pungent	Cows' milk, whole	4-8 weeks
	Brick	United States	Semisoft; smooth, waxy body	Light yellow to orange; brick-shaped; mild	Cows' milk, whole	2 weeks or longer
	Muenster	Germany	Semisoft; smooth, waxy body	Yellow, tan or white surface, creamy white interior; small wheels and blocks; mild to mellow, between brick and Limburger	Cows' milk, whole	2-8 weeks

	CHEESE	ORIGIN	CONSISTENCY AND TEXTURE	COLOR, SHAPE AND FLAVOR	BASIC INGREDIENT	RIPENING PERIOD
Surface-Ripened Family (continued)	Bel Paese	Italy	Soft; smooth, waxy body	Slightly gray surface, creamy yellow interior; small wheels; mild to moderately robust	Cows' milk, whole	6-8 weeks
	Port du Salut (Oka)	Trappist monasteries France and Canada	Semisoft; smooth, buttery	Russet surface, creamy yellow interior; small wheels; mellow to robust, between Cheddar and Limburger	Cows' milk, whole or slightly acid	6-8 weeks
	Limburger	Belgium	Soft; smooth, waxy body	Creamy white; rectangular; robust, highly aromatic	Cows' milk, whole or partly skimmed	1-2 months
Whey Family	Gjetost	Norway	Hard; buttery	Golden brown; cubical and rectangular; sweetish, caramel	Whey from goats' milk	Unripened
	Primost	Norway	Semisoft	Light brown; cubical and cylindrical; mild, sweetish, caramel	Whey with added buttermilk, whole milk or cream	Unripened
	Sapsago	Switzerland	Hard grating; granular	Light green; small, cone-shaped; flavored with clover leaves, sweetish	Cows' milk, skimmed and soured, plus buttermilk and whey	5 months minimum
	Ricotta	Italy	Soft; moist and grainy, or dry	White; packaged fresh in paper, plastic or metal containers or dry for grating; bland, but semisweet	Whey and whole or skim milk, or whole or part skim milk	Unripened

Index